Securing and Troubleshooting Network Operating Systems

EC-Council | Press

Volume 4 of 5 mapping to

E | NSA ™

EC-Council | Network Security
Administrator

Certification

COURSE TECHNOLOGY
CENGAGE Learning™

Australia • Brazil • Japan • Korea • Mexico • Singapore • Spain • United Kingdom • United States

COURSE TECHNOLOGY
CENGAGE Learning™

**Securing and Troubleshooting
Network Operating Systems:
EC-Council | Press**

Course Technology/Cengage Learning
 Staff:

Vice President, Career and Professional
 Editorial: Dave Garza

Director of Learning Solutions:
 Matthew Kane

Executive Editor: Stephen Helba

Managing Editor: Marah Bellegarde

Editorial Assistant: Meghan Orvis

Vice President, Career and Professional
 Marketing: Jennifer Ann Baker

Marketing Director: Deborah Yarnell

Marketing Manager: Erin Coffin

Marketing Coordinator: Shanna Gibbs

Production Director: Carolyn Miller

Production Manager: Andrew Crouth

Content Project Manager:
 Brooke Greenhouse

Senior Art Director: Jack Pendleton

EC-Council:

President | EC-Council: Sanjay Bavisi

Sr. Director US | EC-Council:
 Steven Graham

For product information and technology assistance, contact us at
Cengage Learning Customer & Sales Support, 1-800-354-9706

For permission to use material from this text or product,
submit all requests online at **www.cengage.com/permissions**.
Further permissions questions can be e-mailed to
permissionrequest@cengage.com

Library of Congress Control Number: 2010924639

ISBN-13: 978-1-4354-8358-3

ISBN-10: 1-4354-8358-8

Cengage Learning
5 Maxwell Drive
Clifton Park, NY 12065-2919
USA

Cengage Learning is a leading provider of customized learning solutions with office locations around the globe, including Singapore, the United Kingdom, Australia, Mexico, Brazil, and Japan. Locate your local office at: **international.cengage.com/region**

Cengage Learning products are represented in Canada by
Nelson Education, Ltd.

For more learning solutions, please visit our corporate website at **www.cengage.com**

NOTICE TO THE READER

Printed in the United States of America
1 2 3 4 5 6 7 12 11 10

Brief Table of Contents

Table of Contents

CHAPTER 5

Hacking and electronic crimes sophistication has grown at an exponential rate in recent years. In fact, recent reports have indicated that cyber crime already surpasses the illegal drug trade! Unethical hackers better known as *black hats* are preying on information systems of government, corporate, public, and private networks and are constantly testing the security mechanisms of these organizations to the limit with the sole aim of exploiting it and profiting from the exercise. High profile crimes have proven that the traditional approach to computer security is simply not sufficient, even with the strongest perimeter, properly configured defense mechanisms like firewalls, intrusion detection, and prevention systems, strong end-to-end encryption standards, and anti-virus software. Hackers have proven their dedication and ability to systematically penetrate networks all over the world. In some cases *black hats* may be able to execute attacks so flawlessly that they can compromise a system, steal everything of value, and completely erase their tracks in less than 20 minutes!

The EC-Council Press is dedicated to stopping hackers in their tracks.

About EC-Council

The International Council of Electronic Commerce Consultants, better known as EC-Council was founded in late 2001 to address the need for well-educated and certified information security and e-business practitioners. EC-Council is a global, member-based organization comprised of industry and subject matter experts all working together to set the standards and raise the bar in information security certification and education.

EC-Council first developed the *Certified Ethical Hacker,* C|EH program. The goal of this program is to teach the methodologies, tools, and techniques used by hackers. Leveraging the collective knowledge from hundreds of subject matter experts, the C|EH program has rapidly gained popularity around the globe and is now delivered in over 70 countries by over 450 authorized training centers. Over 80,000 information security practitioners have been trained.

C|EH is the benchmark for many government entities and major corporations around the world. Shortly after C|EH was launched, EC-Council developed the *Certified Security Analyst,* E|CSA. The goal of the E|CSA program is to teach groundbreaking analysis methods that must be applied while conducting advanced penetration testing. E|CSA leads to the *Licensed Penetration Tester,* L|PT status. The *Computer Hacking Forensic Investigator,* C|HFI was formed with the same design methodologies above and has become a global standard in certification for computer forensics. EC-Council through its impervious network of professionals, and huge industry following has developed various other programs in information security and e-business. EC-Council Certifications are viewed as the essential certifications needed where standard configuration and security policy courses fall short. Providing a true, hands-on, tactical approach to security, individuals armed with the knowledge disseminated by EC-Council programs are securing networks around the world and beating the hackers at their own game.

About the EC-Council | Press

The EC-Council | Press was formed in late 2008 as a result of a cutting edge partnership between global information security certification leader, EC-Council and leading global academic publisher, Cengage Learning. This partnership marks a revolution in academic textbooks and courses of study in Information Security, Computer Forensics, Disaster Recovery, and End-User Security. By identifying the essential topics and content of EC-Council professional certification programs, and repurposing this world class content to fit academic programs, the EC-Council | Press was formed. The academic community is now able to incorporate this powerful cutting edge content into new and existing Information Security programs. By closing the gap between academic study and professional certification, students and instructors are able to leverage the power of rigorous academic focus and high demand industry certification. The EC-Council | Press is set to revolutionize global information security programs and ultimately create a new breed of practitioners capable of combating the growing epidemic of cybercrime and the rising threat of cyber-war.

Network Defense Series

The EC-Council | Press *Network Defense* series, preparing learners for E|NSA certification, is intended for those studying to become secure system administrators, network security administrators and anyone who is interested in network security technologies. This series is designed to educate learners, from a vendor neutral standpoint, how to defend the networks they manage. This series covers the fundamental skills in evaluating internal and external threats to network security, design, and how to enforce network level security policies, and ultimately protect an organization's information. Covering a broad range of topics from secure network fundamentals, protocols & analysis, standards and policy, hardening infrastructure, to configuring IPS, IDS and firewalls, bastion host and honeypots, among many other topics, learners completing this series will have a full understanding of defensive measures taken to secure their organizations information. The series when used in its entirety helps prepare readers to take and succeed on the E|N|SA, Network Security Administrator certification exam from EC-Council.

Books in Series
- *Network Defense: Fundamentals and Protocols*/1435483553
- *Network Defense: Security Policy and Threats*/1435483561
- *Network Defense: Perimeter Defense Mechanisms*/143548357X
- *Network Defense: Securing and Troubleshooting Network Operating Systems*/1435483588
- *Network Defense: Security and Vulnerability Assessment*/1435483596

Securing and Troubleshooting Network Operating Systems

Securing and Troubleshooting Network Operating Systems discusses the security of modems, routers, operating systems, patch management, and applications and provides guidance on how to analyze the various logs used to watch for attacks and other important events.

Chapter Contents

Chapter 1 *Securing Modems*, discusses the different types of modems and their features, modem security and a discussion of the different types of modem failures and how to troubleshoot them. Chapter 2, *Hardening Routers*, includes information on how routers work and how to make them more secure. Chapter 3, *Hardening Operating Systems*, familiarizes the reader with how different operating systems handle security and how that security can be increased. Chapter 4, *Patch Management*, discusses how to manage patches for Linux and Windows systems in order to minimize known vulnerabilities. Chapter 5, *Log Analysis*, involves investigating firewall, Web server, system, IDS, and Windows event logs to watch for attacks and other important events. This chapter discusses the different types of logs and how to effectively analyze them. Chapter 6, *Application Security*, discusses the various forms of application security and how to implement them.

Chapter Features

Many features are included in each chapter and all are designed to enhance the learner's learning experience. Features include:

- *Objectives* begin each chapter and focus the learner on the most important concepts in the chapter.

- *Key Terms* are designed to familiarize the learner with terms that will be used within the chapter.

- *Chapter Summary*, at the end of each chapter, serves as a review of the key concepts covered in the chapter.

- *Review Questions* allow the learner to test their comprehension of the chapter content.

- *Hands-On Projects* encourage the learner to apply the knowledge they have gained after finishing the chapter. Files for the *Hands-On Projects* can be found on the Student Resource Center. Note: you will need your access code provided in your book to enter the site. Visit *www.cengage.com/community/eccouncil* for a link to the Student Resource Center.

Student Resource Center

The Student Resource Center contains all the files you need to complete the Hands-On Projects found at the end of the chapters. Access the Student Resource Center with the access code provided in your book. Visit *www.cengage.com/community/eccouncil* for a link to the Student Resource Center.

Additional Instructor Resources

Free to all instructors who adopt the *Securing and Troubleshooting Network Operating Systems* book for their courses is a complete package of instructor resources. These resources are available from the Course Technology web site, *www.cengage.com/coursetechnology*, by going to the product page for this book in the online catalog, and choosing "Instructor Downloads".

Resources include:

- *Instructor Manual*: This manual includes course objectives and additional information to help your instruction.

- *ExamView Testbank*: This Windows-based testing software helps instructors design and administer tests and pre-tests. In addition to generating tests that can be printed and administered, this full-featured program has an online testing component that allows students to take tests at the computer and have their exams automatically graded.

- *PowerPoint Presentations*: This book comes with a set of Microsoft PowerPoint slides for each chapter. These slides are meant to be used as a teaching aid for classroom presentations, to be made available to students for chapter review, or to be printed for classroom distribution. Instructors are also at liberty to add their own slides.

- *Labs*: Additional Hands-on Activities to provide additional practice for your students.

- *Assessment Activities*: Additional assessment opportunities including discussion questions, writing assignments, internet research activities, and homework assignments along with a final cumulative project.

- *Final Exam*: Provides a comprehensive assessment of *Securing and Troubleshooting Network Operating Systems* content.

Cengage Learning Information Security Community Site

This site was created for learners and instructors to find out about the latest in information security news and technology.
Visit *community.cengage.com/infosec* to:

- Learn what's new in information security through live news feeds, videos and podcasts.

- Connect with your peers and security experts through blogs and forums.

- Browse our online catalog.

How to become EINSA Certified

The EINSA certification ensures that the learner has the fundamental skills needed to analyze the internal and external security threats against a network, and to develop security policies that will protect an organization's information. EINSA certified individuals will know how to evaluate network and Internet security issues and design, and how to implement successful security policies and firewall strategies as well as how to expose system and network vulnerabilities and defend against them.
EINSA Certification exams are available through Prometric Prime. To finalize your certification after your training, you must:

1. Purchase an exam voucher from the EC-Council Community Site at Cengage: *www.cengage.com/community/eccouncil.*

2. Speak with your Instructor or Professor about scheduling an exam session, or visit the EC-Council Community Site referenced above for more information.

3. Take and pass the EINSA certification examination with a score of 70% or better.

About Our Other EC-Council | Press Products

Ethical Hacking and Countermeasures Series

The EC-Council | Press *Ethical Hacking and Countermeasures* series is intended for those studying to become security officers, auditors, security professionals, site administrators, and anyone who is concerned about or responsible for the integrity of the network infrastructure. The series includes a broad base of topics in offensive network security, ethical hacking, as well as network defense and countermeasures. The content of this series is designed to immerse the learner into an interactive environment where they will be shown how to scan, test, hack and secure information systems. A wide variety of tools, viruses, and malware is presented in these books, providing a complete understanding of the tactics and tools used by hackers. By gaining a thorough understanding of how hackers operate, ethical hackers are able to set up strong countermeasures and defensive systems to protect their organization's critical infrastructure and information. The series when used in its entirety helps prepare readers to take and succeed on the C|EH certification exam from EC-Council.

Books in Series:
* *Ethical Hacking and Countermeasures: Attack Phases*/143548360X
* *Ethical Hacking and Countermeasures: Threats and Defense Mechanisms*/1435483618
* *Ethical Hacking and Countermeasures: Web Applications and Data Servers*/1435483626
* *Ethical Hacking and Countermeasures: Linux, Macintosh and Mobile Systems*/1435483642
* *Ethical Hacking and Countermeasures: Secure Network Infrastructures*/1435483650

Computer Forensics Series

The EC-Council | Press *Computer Forensics* series, preparing learners for C|HFI certification, is intended for those studying to become police investigators and other law enforcement personnel, defense and military personnel, e-business security professionals, systems administrators, legal professionals, banking, insurance and other professionals, government agencies, and IT managers. The content of this program is designed to expose the learner to the process of detecting attacks and collecting evidence in a forensically sound manner with the intent to report crime and prevent future attacks. Advanced techniques in computer investigation and analysis with interest in generating potential legal evidence are included. In full, this series prepares the learner to identify evidence in computer related crime and abuse cases as well as track the intrusive hacker's path through client system.

Books in Series:
* *Computer Forensics: Investigation Procedures and Response*/1435483499
* *Computer Forensics: Investigating Hard Disks, File and Operating Systems*/1435483502
* *Computer Forensics: Investigating Data and Image Files*/1435483510
* *Computer Forensics: Investigating Network Intrusions and Cybercrime*/1435483529
* *Computer Forensics: Investigating Wireless Networks and Devices*/1435483537

Pentration Testing Series

The EC-Council | Press *Security Analyst/Licensed Penetration Tester* series, preparing learners for E|CSA/LPT certification, is intended for those studying to become Network Server Administrators, Firewall Administrators, Security Testers, System Administrators and Risk Assessment professionals. This series covers a broad base of topics in advanced penetration testing and security analysis. The content of this program is designed to expose the learner to groundbreaking methodologies in conducting thorough security analysis, as well as advanced penetration testing techniques. Armed with the knowledge from the Security Analyst series, learners will be able to perform the intensive assessments required to effectively identify and mitigate risks to the security of the organization's infrastructure. The series when used in its entirety helps prepare readers to take and succeed on the E|CSA, Certified Security Analyst certification exam.

E|CSA certification is a relevant milestone towards achieving EC-Council's Licensed Penetration Tester (LPT) designation, which also ingrains the learner in the business aspect of penetration testing. To learn more about this designation please visit http://www.eccouncil.org/lpt.htm.

Books in Series:
* *Penetration Testing: Security Analysis*/1435483669
* *Penetration Testing: Procedures and Methodologies*/1435483677
* *Penetration Testing: Network and Perimeter Testing*/1435483685
* *Penetration Testing: Communication Media Testing*/1435483693
* *Penetration Testing: Network Threat Testing* /1435483707

Cyber Safety/1435483715

Cyber Safety is designed for anyone who is interested in learning computer networking and security basics. This product provides information cyber crime; security procedures; how to recognize security threats and attacks, incident response, and how to secure internet access. This book gives individuals the basic security literacy skills to begin high-end IT programs. The book also prepares readers to take and succeed on the Security|5 certification exam from EC-Council.

Wireless Safety/1435483766

Wireless Safety introduces the learner to the basics of wireless technologies and its practical adaptation. *Wireless|5* is tailored to cater to any individual's desire to learn more about wireless technology. It requires no pre-requisite knowledge and aims to educate the learner in simple applications of these technologies. Topics include wireless signal propagation, IEEE and ETSI Wireless Standards, WLANs and Operation, Wireless Protocols and Communication Languages, Wireless Devices, and Wireless Security Network. The book also prepares readers to take and succeed on the Wireless|5 certification exam from EC-Council.

Network Safety/1435483774

Network Safety provides the basic core knowledge on how infrastructure enables a working environment. Intended for those in an office environment and for the home user who wants to optimize resource utilization, share infrastructure and make the best of technology and the convenience it offers. Topics include foundations of networks, networking components, wireless networks, basic hardware components, the networking environment and connectivity as well as troubleshooting. The book also prepares readers to take and succeed on the Network|5 certification exam from EC-Council.

Disaster Recovery Series

The *Disaster Recovery Series* is designed to fortify virtualization technology knowledge of system administrators, systems engineers, enterprise system architects, and any IT professional who is concerned about the integrity of the their network infrastructure. Virtualization technology gives the advantage of additional flexibility as well as cost savings while deploying a disaster recovery solution. The series when used in its entirety helps prepare readers to take and succeed on the E|CDR and E|CVT, Disaster Recovery and Virtualization Technology certification exam from EC-Council. The EC-Council Certified Disaster Recovery and Virtualization Technology professional will have a better understanding of how to setup Disaster Recovery Plans using traditional and virtual technologies to ensure business continuity in the event of a disaster.

Books in Series
- *Disaster Recovery* /1435488709
- *Virtualization Security*/1435488695

Acknowledgements

Michael H. Goldner is the Chair of the School of Information Technology for ITT Technical Institute in Norfolk Virginia, and also teaches bachelor level courses in computer network and information security systems. Michael has served on and chaired ITT Educational Services Inc. National Curriculum Committee on Information Security. He received his Juris Doctorate from Stetson University College of Law, his undergraduate degree from Miami University and has been working over fifteen years in the area of Information Technology. He is an active member of the American Bar Association, and has served on that organization's Cyber Law committee. He is a member of IEEE, ACM and ISSA, and is the holder of a number of industrially recognized certifications including, CISSP, CEH, CHFI, CEI, MCT, MCSE/Security, Security +, Network + and A+. Michael recently completed the design and creation of a computer forensic program for ITT Technical Institute, and has worked closely with both EC Council and Delmar/Cengage Learning in the creation of this EC Council Press series.

Chapter 1

Securing Modems

Objectives

After completing this chapter, you should be able to:

- Understand the origin and features of modems
- Describe the different types of modems
- Understand modem security
- Understand modem risks and attacks
- Understand the different types of modem failures
- Troubleshoot modems

Key Terms

Call forwarding   the process of forwarding an incoming unanswered or busy-signal call from direct inward dial (DID) trunks, tie lines, and 800 services to outside lines or long-distance facilities, with call charges billed to the PBX owner or service subscriber

Modem   a device that allows two computers to communicate, often via a standard telephone line, by converting an analog signal into a digital signal and vice versa

Universal asynchronous receiver/transmitter (UART)   computer hardware that translates data between parallel and serial forms

Wardialing   the process of automatically dialing multiple telephone numbers in search of open insecure modems

Introduction to Securing Modems

This chapter focuses on securing modems. It begins by discussing the origin and features of modems. It also covers the different types of modems. The chapter then continues on to modem security, including modem risks and the attacks launched against modems. It finishes with a discussion of the different types of modem failures and how to troubleshoot them.

Introduction to Modems

A *modem* is a device that allows two computers to communicate, often via a standard telephone line. The word *modem* comes from the words *modulator* and *demodulator*. The function of a modem is to convert digital data into analog signals and convert analog signals back into digital data. Modems come in different sizes and shapes.

Origin and Description of Modems

On a network, the modem at the sender's side modulates the data into a signal that is compatible with the phone line; another modem on the receiving side demodulates the signal back into digital data.

Modems came into use in the 1960s as a way to allow terminals to connect computers through the phone line. In the simplest configuration, a dumb terminal can dial into a central computer. The 1960s were an age for time-shared computers; businesses would often buy computer time from a time-shared facility and connect to it via a 300 bits per second (bps) modem.

When personal computers started gaining wide acceptance in the late 1970s, bulletin board systems (BBSs) became the rage. A person set up a computer with a modem and some BBS software, and other people would dial in to connect to the bulletin board.

People got along at 300 bps for quite a while. The reason this speed was acceptable was because 300 bps represents about 30 characters per second, which is a lot more characters per second than a person can type or read. Once people started transferring large programs and images to and from bulletin board systems, however, 300 bps became impractical. Modem speeds went through the following steps:

- 300 bps: 1960s through approximately 1983
- 1200 bps: Gained popularity in 1984 and 1985
- 2400 bps
- 9600 bps: First appeared in late 1990 and early 1991
- 19.2 kilobits per second (Kbps)
- 28.8 Kbps
- 33.6 Kbps
- 56 Kbps: Became the standard in 1998
- ADSL, with a theoretical maximum speed of 8 megabits per second (Mbps): Gained popularity in 1999

Modem Features

The following are some of the main features of modems:

- *Modems convert data from analog to digital and vice versa*: A modem converts analog data to digital and vice versa. Users can also use modems as telephones to make calls from their PCs with the use of speakers and a microphone.
- *Speed capabilities of a modem*: Modem speeds are typically measured in bits per second (bps) or kilobits per second (Kbps). Dial-up modems range from 300 bps to 56 Kbps.
- *Dial-up modems can achieve higher transfer rates*: A modem has the facility to compress data to allow for higher data transfer rates. Many Internet providers can offer high speed Internet by compressing the information before transferring it through the phone line.

Types of Modems

The following are the two basic types of modems:

1. *External modems*: This modem resides outside the computer, and is connected to the serial port by a cable and to the telephone wall jack by another cable.
2. *Internal modems*: This type of modem is installed in the computer. It is connected to the telephone wall jack by a cable.

The other types of modems include the following:

- Internal direct-connect modems
- External direct-connect modems
- Optical modems
- Short-haul modems
- Controller-less modems
- Acoustic modems
- Null modem cables

Internal Direct-Connect Modems

This type of modem consists of an IC (integrated circuit) board or card that is installed in a computer's expansion slot. An internal direct-connect modem contains a modular jack for connecting the modem to a telephone line.

Advantages and Disadvantages of Internal Direct-Connect Modems

The installation of an internal modem requires no cables, and this type of modem is less vulnerable to external disturbance. Using an internal modem in a laptop means one less piece of hardware to carry, and it does not require external electrical power, becaue it takes power from its host computer's power supply.

One disadvantage of an internal modem is that it is an integral part of the computer and works only with the system for which it is designed. Another disadvantage is that the user cannot easily monitor the call's status through an external indicator.

External Direct-Connect Modems

This type of modem has a power line, one or two modular jacks, and an RS-232C connector. The RS-232C connector, which is used to connect to the computer's serial port, is usually situated at the back of the modem. The front of the modem contains lights that indicate the modem's operation and call status.

Advantages and Disadvantages of External Direct-Connect Modems

One advantage that an external modem has over an internal modem is that it can be used in more than one kind of computer. Another advantage of this modem is that if the modem needs repair, it can be uninstalled without opening the computer up. Also, because it is external, accessing DIP switches and setting them is very easy. This modem contains status lights that are used to monitor the modem's operation and call status, making it easier for users to perform troubleshooting. One disadvantage of this type of modem is that it needs an external power source. External modems are also typically bigger and heavier than their internal counterparts.

Optical Modems

This type of modem provides higher data-transmission rates compared with other modems because data are transmitted over high-capacity optical fiber cables. This modem converts digital signals into optical signals for transmission over the optical fiber, and it converts the optical signals back into digital signals for the computer's use.

Short-Haul Modems

Short-haul modems can be used in applications where a serial connection is needed over short distances, such as for a weather station or data logger.

The following are some applications short-haul modems support:

- They are used for point-to-point extensions of enterprise and education networks over short distances, including LAN and T1 extensions.
- SONET (synchronous optical network) extensions from the ADM (add/drop multiplexer) use xDSL technology to deliver high capacity circuits to the last mile and within buildings.

Controller-Less Modems

This modem is implemented as a virtual device driver, with all processing handled by the host computer to remove the need for a standalone processor for the modem. The virtual device driver ensures the modem gets sufficient processing time regardless of other processes running on the host. Merging a driver directly into the contact code, the need for hardware UART with its attendant limitations is reduced. *UART (universal asynchronous receiver/transmitter)* is computer hardware that translates data between parallel and serial forms.

Acoustic Modems

This modem is used to transmit data underwater, in a manner similar to how telephone modems transmit data via a telephone cable. This modem converts digital data into special underwater sound signals and vice versa. This modem can be used for applications that are required in underwater wireless communications, such as underwater telemetry, diver communications, underwater monitoring, data logging, and ROV and AUV command and control (an ROV is an underwater rover, and an AUV is an autonomous underwater vehicle).

Advantages and Disadvantages of Acoustic Modems

These modems are less expensive than a direct-connect modem and require no special plugs or outlets. They are suitable to use with hardwired hotel or pay telephones. The disadvantage of an acoustic modem is that it requires manual operation (i.e., you must dial the telephone number and listen for the remote system to answer, hang up the telephone manually, etc.). These modems are less popular than direct-connect modems.

Null Modem Cables

A null modem cable is used to connect one PC to another PC or serial device by using modem protocols. The null modem cable can also be used to set up head-to-head gaming between two players at different computers in the same room. (A null modem cable is limited to 30 feet in length.)

Modem Security

Modems introduce a number of security problems because they create a link between a computer and the outside world. An organization's employees use modems to access confidential information, but attackers can use modems to attempt to access the same information.

There are many ways to protect an organization's modems. An administrator should place the modems in a secure location so that unauthorized persons cannot use them. This protection prevents the modem from being altered. Many modems allow remote configuration and testing. This facility makes changes simpler for personnel who manage different remote locations. It also makes it easy for an attacker to use, so administrators should be careful. If a modem has such a feature and there is a chance that it will be compromised, the administrator should disable that feature.

Another important security aspect is protecting telephone numbers. Making the telephone numbers for modems widely known increases the chance that someone might try to use them to break into the system.

Additional Security for Modems

If a modem is connected to an outside telephone line, then anyone can call it. Usernames and password are more important security aspects for modems. However, sometimes even a good password can be guessed or discovered by others. To protect usernames and passwords, modems with additional security features have been developed.

Password Modems

These modems require a password from the caller when the modem connects the caller to a computer. These modems provide security to attempt to protect the system from unauthorized users. Normally, this type of modem stores one to 10 passwords.

Callback Modems

Using a callback modem is the safest technique to prevent unauthorized access through modems. When a user connects to this type of modem, it hangs up and checks a list of valid users and their telephone numbers before calling the user back to establish the call. These modems are very expensive, so this is not a practical solution for many systems.

Encrypting Modems

These modems encrypt all information transmitted over the telephone line. These modems provide high security, not only against users who are attempting unauthorized access, but also against those who are performing wiretapping.

Caller-ID and ANI Schemes

Caller-ID or ANI (automatic number identification) can be used as a form of access control. The Caller-ID or ANI information is compared with a list of authorized phone numbers when the user calls the modem. If the number is valid, then the call is switched to the computer.

Categorizing Modem Access

Dial-Out Access

In dial-out access, internal users connect to an external system, typically an ISP. In this type of access, users dial out through a modem to an external ISP, which provide a direct two-way connection. The main risk with this access is that it is mainly used for Internet access and allows unrestricted service to the following:

- Unauthorized software, such as Trojan horses or viruses
- Gaming servers
- Copyrighted and offensive material

Dial-In Access

In dial-in access, external users dial in and connect to one of the organization's internal systems. The following are some of the potential risks associated with dial-in (remote) access:

- Allowing access to an organization's internal machines
- Allowing access to affiliated networks
- Allowing access to sensitive information

Modem Attacks and Risks

Modem Attacks

Spoofing Attacks

Through a spoofing attack, an attacker aims to create a context that misleads the victim into making bad security-related decisions. Spoofing attacks are possible in the material world as well as the electronic one. For example, criminals set up fake automated teller machines, normally in the vicinity of shopping malls. The machines accept ATM cards and request the person to enter his or her PIN. As soon as the machine gets the victim's PIN, it corrupts and returns the card. In such a case, the criminals have adequate information to duplicate the victim's card. In these attacks, people are deceived by the context they see: the position of the machines, their size and weight, and the appearance of their electronic displays.

Computer users generally make security decisions depending on the situation. For instance, if a user is visiting an Internet banking site, he or she feels confident when entering his or her account number because he or she assumes the bank's Web page is authentic. He or she feels this way because the bank's URL appears in the browser's address bar, the bank's logo appears on the Web site, along with other contextual details. However, the user could be a victim of an online spoofing attack.

The following are some ways to combat spoofing attacks:

- JavaScript in a user's browser must be disabled so the attacker will be unable to conceal the proof of the attack.
- Users must ensure that the browser's address bar is always visible.
- Users must pay attention to the URLs displayed in the browser's address bar, ensuring that they always indicate the server they are supposed to be connected to.
- Administrators should set up packet filtering to block unauthorized data packets.

Call-Forwarding Attacks

Call forwarding is a serious threat in modem attacks. Forwarding an incoming unanswered or busy-signal call from direct inward dial (DID) trunks, tie lines, and 800 services to outside lines or long-distance facilities with call charges billed to the PBX owner or service subscriber is called *call forwarding*.

Call-forwarding features are also used within companies during business hours to implement transfers of unanswered calls from employee to employee. Employees often abuse this feature by forwarding business phones to their home phones or their relatives' phones. Hackers can also reprogram this system to forward calls and allow them to hide behind the victim's PBX, which may make it difficult to track the calls.

Wardialing

Wardialing is the process of automatically dialing multiple telephone numbers in search of open insecure modems. It involves dialing a block of numbers from a publicly switched telephone network (PSTN) (e.g., 238-0064 to 238-5020) in an attempt to track carrier signals or other different tones that may exist in an organization's private branch exchange (PBX) or phone system. Most profitable wardialers' telephone-line scanner applications sense not only modems but also fax lines, voice lines, busy tones, and abnormalities that may be present in the organization's PBX system.

A common technique is to discover one telephone number a target owns and then to wardial all numbers using that same prefix. Wardialing one telephone number takes around 35 seconds. This means that wardialing 10,000 numbers would take a maximum of four days.

The following are some popular wardialing tools:

- ToneLoc
- SecureLogix Telesweep Secure
- Sandstorm PhoneSweep

Modem Risks

Packet Sniffing

A packet sniffer is a program that monitors packets being transmitted over a network. In a shared Ethernet environment, all hosts are linked to the same bus and contend with one another for bandwidth. In this environment, packets destined for one machine pass through every machine on the network. Some basic packet sniffers use a command-line interface and dump captured data to the screen, while advanced packet sniffers use a GUI, graph traffic figures, detect numerous sessions, and offer a number of design options. Network analysis programs often use sniffers to collect data essential for metrics and investigation. Sniffers typically do not alter the captured data.

Modem Failures

Modem Firmware Failure

Modems are controlled by code called firmware that resides inside the modem itself, and this code can be changed and updated. Sometimes, this code is stored in programmable read-only memory (PROM) integrated circuits. Modem manufacturers update their firmware occasionally to add new features or to fix problems. When the code is changed, it is necessary to replace the PROM chip. The latest modems store the code in flash memory, which is a nonvolatile type of memory like PROMs. The benefit of using flash memory is that the code can be updated without changing the hardware. If a modem is having a problem, users should first check to make sure they have the latest firmware. Also, it could be possible that the firmware update procedure went wrong, so users should try updating the firmware again.

Reasons for Modem Connection Failures

Modem Incompatibilities

With the use of new technologies, many modems are not fully compatible. There are cases where two different modems can connect but not at the speed and options desired. Sometimes, the reported speed of the modem is less than the desired or required speed.

Bad Phone Line

There are many cases where phone-line problems occur. The latest modems adjust the speed automatically according to the line quality. When the speed is consistently lower than the advertised speed, users should install new drivers or firmware, if available. Users can also either test the phone line themselves or call the phone company to have the company test the line.

Temporary Modem Failures

There are times that modems fail for no apparent reason. The solution is usually to reset the modem or power it down. Some modems reset automatically after each call.

Other Common Failures

The following are some other common modem failures:

- *Modem not responding*: When the modem is not responding, there may be a reason as simple as the wrong jack being used or another program using the serial port, or it could be a serious hardware issue. The following are steps a user can take to try to fix the problem:
  - *Power cycle*: When the error first occurs power cycle the computer and modem.
  - *Check the phone line and remove devices*: Check whether the phone is off the hook or if any other device is using the line, such as an answering machine, a spike block, or a call zapper.
  - *Check that the modem is plugged in correctly*: Check that the modem cable is plugged into the correct port on the modem. Also, check that the cable is securely plugged into the wall jack.
  - *Correct modem selected in connection*: In Windows, verify the dial-up networking connection and make sure that the correct modem is selected for the connection.
- *Modem damaged*: To find out whether the modem is damaged, first disconnect the phone line from the modem and reconnect it. If it is still not working, that means the modem may have been damaged. Connect a telephone to the telephone jack of the modem and check that the modem can get a dial tone. Then check whether the modem lights are functioning properly.

Troubleshooting Modems

External Modems

The following are the three connections of interest when troubleshooting an external modem:

1. Power connection between modem and wall outlet
2. Data cable between modem and computer
3. Phone plug connected to phone system and computer

A user should check all three to make sure they are all properly connected.

The Data Cable

A serial data cable has a male DB-25 plug on one end and a female DB-25 plug on the other end. This cable connects the external modem to the computer's serial port.

The Power Cable

The user should plug the round end of the power supply into the rear of the modem in the appropriate jack and plug the other end into the power outlet. When the modem is properly connected to the power outlet, at least one of the modem's lights will blink.

The Phone Line

One end of the phone line should be connected to the modem, and the other end should be connected to the wall jack. If either is not securely plugged in, the modem will not work properly.

Internal Modems

Installation Issues

Users should make sure the modem is seated properly in the expansion slot. Internal modems also require software drivers, so users should make sure they install the correct driver for their modem.

The Phone Line

Users should make sure the phone line is securely connected to both the modem and the wall jack. Sometimes, other parts get in the way and prevent a secure connection to the modem. Also, some modems have a pass-through connection that allows users to connect a telephone to the modem, so they should make sure the phone line is connected to the correct port on the modem.

Hardware Settings

Users should check the current hardware Interrupt Request (IRQ) settings. Two devices cannot use the same IRQ, so if the modem is using the same IRQ as another device, users should change one of the conflicting IRQs.

Chapter Summary

- A modem is a device that allows two computers to communicate, often via a standard telephone line.
- On the network, the modem at the sender's side modulates the data into a signal that is compatible with the phone line; another modem on the receiving side demodulates the signal back into digital data.
- The two basic types of modems are external modems and internal modems.
- In dial-out access, internal users connect to an external system, typically an ISP.
- In dial-in access, external users dial in and connect to one of the organization's internal systems.
- Through a spoofing attack, an attacker aims to create a context that misleads the victim into making bad security-related decisions.
- Modem failures can be related to either hardware or software.

Review Questions

1. What is a modem?

   _____

   _____

   _____

   _____

2. List the differences between an internal direct-connect modem and an external direct-connect modem.

3. What is a short-haul modem?

4. How does an acoustic modem work?

5. What is a null modem cable and how is one used?

6. How does a password modem work?

7. How does a callback modem work?

8. What is a spoofing attack?

9. What is a call-forwarding attack?

_____

_____

_____

_____

10. What is wardialing?

_____

_____

_____

_____

11. List the reasons for modem connection failures.

_____

_____

_____

_____

12. Describe some steps a user can take to try to fix a modem that is not responding.

_____

_____

_____

_____

13. How do you troubleshoot external modems?

_____

_____

_____

14. How do you troubleshoot internal modems?

_____

_____

_____

_____

Hands-On Projects

1. Navigate to Chapter 1 of the Student Resource Center and open Securing Control Systems Modems.pdf. Read the following topics:

   ■ IP versus Modem Security

   ■ Modem Security Methods

2. Navigate to Chapter 1 of the Student Resource Center and open Modem Threats.pdf. Read the following topics:

   ▪ Modems – The Overlooked Threat

   ▪ Ethical Use of PhoneSweep

3. Navigate to Chapter 1 of the Student Resource Center and open Modem Security.pdf. Read the following topics:

   ▪ OBM (Out of Band Management) Overview

   ▪ OBM Modem Security

4. Navigate to Chapter 1 of the Student Resource Center and open Modem Security Policy.pdf. Read the following topics:

   ▪ Modem Security Policy

   ▪ Responsibilities

Chapter 2

Hardening Routers

Objectives

After completing this chapter, you should be able to:

- Understand routers, metrics, algorithms, and IOS
- Understand routing principles and operation modes
- Understand IP routing
- Configure routers
- Understanding TCP and UDP small servers and various tools
- Harden routers
- Understand the Cisco discovery protocol
- Implement access control lists
- Secure routers
- Understand router commands, router types, and routing protocols
- Troubleshoot routers

Key Terms

Least-cost routing   the strategy of directing a packet through the shortest route possible

Routing table   a table containing the paths for the routing of data packets

Introduction to Hardening Routers

In packet-switched networks such as the Internet, a router is a piece of hardware or software that determines the next network point to which a packet should be forwarded. The router is connected to at least two networks, as shown in Figure 2-1, and it decides which way to send each information packet, based on its current understanding of the state of the networks. It is located at any gateway (where one network meets another), including each point-of-presence on the Internet. Routers are often included as a part of network switches.

This chapter will familiarize you with how routers work and teach you how to make them more secure.

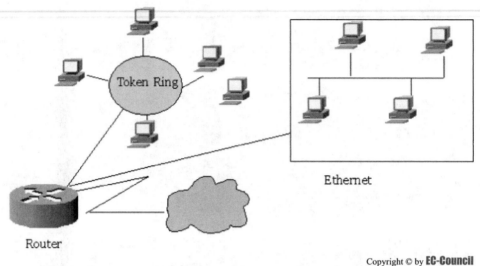

Figure 2-1   Routers are connected to at least two networks.

Router Basics

A router can link networks that have dissimilar protocols and topologies. They can access the addresses of the network layer and can include software that helps them to identify which channel is appropriate for the transmission of data.

Routers function in the physical, data-link, and network layers of the OSI model. If there is no router between the sender and receiver, the sender must transmit the packets directly to the destination. If a received packet contains the address of a node of a network that is not connected to the router, the router will identify which of the linked networks is the next-best option.

A router maintains a *routing table*, containing the paths for the routing of data packets as well as the cost of routing across the network. The network administrator can monitor routing processes if static routing is enabled.

Routers try to find the shortest route for their packets, which is a concept known as *least-cost routing*. This path should be both secure and fast. Some routers are also capable of routing packets across networks that use more than one protocol.

Routing Metrics

A metric is a standard for assessing routes in a network. Routers calculate the best route by making use of one or more metrics. Metrics frequently used by routers include the following:

- *Hop count*: This is the most popular metric used by routers. It denotes the number of times a packet passes through an intermediary device to reach the destination node.

- *Latency*: Latency refers to the amount of time it takes to route a packet from the source node to the destination node. Latency is dependent on many factors, such as traffic load and the bandwidth of the channel or link.

- *Bandwidth*: Bandwidth refers to the capacity of a channel or link, stated in megabits or megabytes per second. Higher bandwidth means a faster network.

- *Tick*: One tick is equal to a delay of one-eighth of a second.

- *Cost*: Cost refers to the functioning cost of the link, which includes the number of hops, the latency of each hop, and the bandwidth of the route or routes used. It would be assumed that a T1 line would have a lower cost using this transmission than a modem line, but if there is congestion on the T1 line, it could be more cost effective to use the modem line. The total cost is the sum of all the factors involved in moving the data from the source to the destination.

- *Load*: Load refers to how hectic the network is with its resources. Load is estimated in terms of CPU usage and packets processed per second.

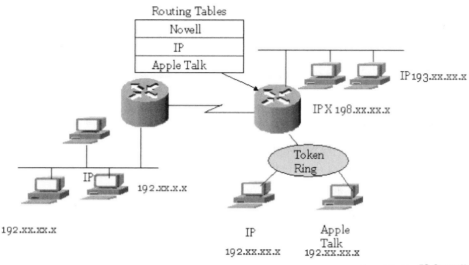

Figure 2-2   Multiprotocol routing sees one router handling different protocols simultaneously.

Multiprotocol Routing

Multiprotocol routing, shown in Figure 2-2, is a type of routing in which a single router supports several different protocols, such as IP and IPX, and maintains different routing tables for each protocol.

Types of Routes

The router can be set to use several different types of routes, including the following:

- *Static routes*: Static routes are manually configured point-to-point routes. Because the routes are manually specified, the administrator has to keep track of every change in the network.

- *Dynamic routes*: Dynamic routes are updated automatically. A router configured with dynamic routes keeps track of all the changes in the network and adjusts the routing table accordingly.

- *Default routes*: Defined in the routing table of the router, a default route is a path on which a packet is transmitted when no definite path is available for the destination node.

Routing Algorithms

Available routing algorithms include the following:

- *Distance-vector algorithms*: These algorithms are also called *Bellman-Ford algorithms*. Routers interact with neighboring routers and transfer copies of routing tables. This helps the routers learn the topology of the network and update their own routing tables. Examples of these protocols include Routing Information Protocol (RIP) and Interior Gateway Routing Protocol (IGRP).

- *Link-state algorithms*: Link-state algorithms are also known as shortest-path-first algorithms. They broadcast routing information to all nodes in the network and maintain a complex database of topology information. These algorithms also contain a full knowledge of distance routers. Common protocols include Open Shortest Path First (OSPF) and NetWare Link Services Protocol (NLSP).

- *Hybrid algorithms*: Hybrid algorithms combine both distance-vector and link-state algorithms. These algorithms use distance-vector algorithms to determine the best path to the destination node and link-state algorithms with increased bandwidth to determine the cost of a link. Examples of such algorithms include Enhanced Interior Gateway Routing Protocol (EIGRP) and Intermediate System to Intermediate System (IS-IS).

Distance-Vector Routing

The distance vector determines how many hops away the destination is from the source and selects the path with the lowest distance value. The distance value is represented by hops or a combination of metrics. Each router uses echo packets to determine its distance from each of its neighbors. The distance-vector routing protocol works as follows:

1. The router first makes a routing table of the entire network it can reach and how many hops it will take to reach each node.

2. The routing table is shared with other routers in a given interval of time.

3. The routers construct a new routing table based on the network interfaces and the information received from the other routers.

4. Bad paths are deleted. If two ideal paths exist, then the one with the smallest hop count is taken.

5. The new routing table is then forwarded to all the neighbors of the router.

The following are some of the problems with distance-vector routing:

- *Same-neighbor problem*: Two neighboring router nodes would have the exact same routing path information.

- *Counting to infinity*: If one node goes down, a situation can occur in which the routing algorithm gives incorrect information to a neighboring router because it is unaware that one link in the route is down. In this case, the data never reach their destination.

- *Routing loops*: This is a situation in which the routing algorithm within a group of nodes forms a loop, delaying or stopping the data from reaching the ultimate destination.

- *Hold down timer*: This is a situation in which a node refuses route updates for a few minutes after a route retraction, which eliminates the routing-loop problem but causes a large increase in convergence times.

Link-State Routing

The link-state routing protocol uses the LSA algorithm for the communication of routing information to other routers. Each router has a topology database in its buffer. A link-state router only notifies the neighboring router when any change occurs.

Cisco Internetwork Operating System (IOS)

Cisco IOS is designed for the configuration of Cisco network devices, such as routers and switches. IOS is the software running internally on Cisco's routers and higher-end switches. It also includes all the hardware-specific drivers required for the devices, as well as all the specifications and commands needed for configuring the network with the devices.

IOS enhances network performance and supports network applications such as firewalls, NAT, DHCP, file system managers, telnet, FTP, HTTP, TFTP, multimedia voice managers, multimedia conference managers, debugging tools, and more.

Features of IOS

The networking features of Cisco IOS are primarily based on international standards, permitting Cisco products to interoperate with disparate media and devices across an enterprise network.

Scalability

Cisco IOS software utilizes international standards to prevent congestion by scalable routing protocols that permit the network to avoid limits to the network and protocols' architectures. It uses filters to reduce extraneous protocol traffic and network broadcasts through timers and helper addresses. It reduces the network traffic overhead, thus maintaining an efficient and effective network infrastructure.

Adaptability

Routing protocols help the router decide the optimum path along which to send the data packets during a power outage, ensuring the reliable delivery of information. Packet prioritization and services enable Cisco routers to account for constraints on bandwidth. IOS software preserves bandwidth and maintains the performance of the network while balancing traffic throughput.

Access Support

The Cisco IOS software supports remote access and protocol translation services that provide connectivity to the following:

- Terminals
- Modems
- Computers
- Printers
- Workstations

Many network configurations exist for connecting these network resources over local area networks (LANs) and wide area networks (WANs). LAN terminal service supports the following:

- TCP/IP support for telnet and rlogin connections to IP hosts
- TN3270 connections to IBM hosts
- LAT connections to DEC hosts

Performance Optimization

Network devices must be able to readily make decisions on routing packets in a cost-effective manner.

Dial-On-Demand Access (DDA)

DDA is useful in regard to the following:

- Dial-up backup
- Dynamic bandwidth

An effective network design must have a backup solution for telecommunications outages. A router should be able to sense the outage of a line and create a dial-up connection over the switched serial, ISDN, T1, or frame relay. This way, an organization can maintain connectivity to the WAN with minimal downtime. The DDA function monitors the primary activation line and cuts the connection automatically, if required. DDA identifies a low- and high-bandwidth watermark on the permanent lines, allowing the addition of a temporary connection to another location to meet throughput and performance criteria.

Dial-On-Demand Routing (DDR)

DDR permits Cisco routers to create temporary WAN connections using packets such as IP, Novell IPX, X.25, Frame Relay, and SMDS. When the router detects such a packet, dial-up connections are secured to a definite packet that relates to the DDR configuration. This way, connectivity to remote locations is provided on a temporary basis, reducing the cost of network connectivity.

Security

In addition to simple firewalling, Cisco IOS classifies networks and restricts access to high-security server networks. IOS facilitates encryption, authenticates dial-in access, requires permissions on changing configurations, and provides accounting and logging to identify unauthorized access. It also supports standard authentication packages like RADIUS and TACACS+ for access to the router. IOS requires user authentication for router access and provides multilevel access to IOS command interface functions.

Routing Principles

Routing is the function used to locate the best path from the source to the destination. When the target is on the local network, the Address Resolution Protocol (ARP) is used to identify the MAC of the target host and the transmitted datagram.

When the target host is not on the local network, it is directed to the router. The router then checks the routing table to determine the best route for the packet. If multiple routes exist, the router makes a decision about the best path.

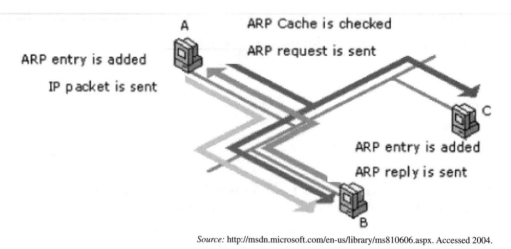

Source: http://msdn.microsoft.com/en-us/library/ms810606.aspx. Accessed 2004.

Figure 2-3 ARP identifies the MAC address of the target host.

ARP Process

ARP gets the IP packet, the destination address of the packet, and the interface used to forward the packet. Whether the delivery of the packets is direct or indirect, ARP uses the following process, shown in Figure 2-3:

1. ARP consults the ARP cache, where an entry for forwarding the IP address may be stored.
2. If an entry is found, ARP forwards the packet to the host.
3. If an entry is not found, ARP builds an ARP request frame containing the MAC address of the interface sending the ARP request.
4. ARP then broadcasts the ARP request using the proper interface.
5. All hosts receive and process the ARP request frame.
6. If the receiving host's IP address matches the requested IP address, the ARP cache is updated.
7. If the receiving host's IP does not match the requested IP address, the ARP request is discarded.
8. The ARP reply contains the requested MAC address and is sent directly to the sender of the ARP request.
9. After the ARP reply is received by the sender of the ARP request, the ARP cache is updated with the address mapping.
10. Both hosts now have each other's address mapped in their ARP cache.
11. The IP packets are then sent to the host's MAC address, which is done by addressing the packets to the resolved MAC address.

Configuring Routers

IP Routing

Administrative Distance Values

Administrative distance specifies the reliability of a routing information source, denoted as an integer between 0 and 255. Zero indicates that the route is extremely reliable, and 255 indicates that the route is not reliable at all.

Directly linked interfaces are always reliable and have an administrative distance of 0. Static routes have an administrative distance of 1. If the route source is unknown, the administrative distance is 255. Routes using RIP (discussed later) have an administrative distance of 120.

Configuring Static Routes

Static routes are physically described. To configure static routes, the following command can be executed in IOS from global configuration mode:

```
ip route <network address> <subnet mask> {IP address |interface}
[administrative distance]
```

The following are the parameters for this command:

- *network address*: Destination network address
- *subnet mask*: Subnet mask of the destination address
- *IP address*: IP address of the next-hop router
- *interface*: Name of interface used to link to the destination network
- *administrative distance*: Integer from 0 to 255 indicating the trustworthiness of a routing source

For example:

```
ip route 192.168.10.1 255.255.255.0 192.168.11.10
```

Configuring IP and IP Routing

An IP can be configured for each interface of the router by allocating an IP address. To assign an IP address to an interface, the following command is used:

```
ip address <ip address> <subnet mask>
```

The above command assigns an IP address to an interface. For example, to configure the Ethernet interface of a router:

```
int e0
```

```
ip address 192.168.12.12 255.255.255.0
```

```
no shutdown
```

The above example configures the Ethernet interface of a router at IP address 192.168.12.12 with the default subnet mask, 255.255.255.0. After assigning the IP address to an interface, the **no shutdown** command must be executed to activate the interface.

After configuring the IP address for the interface of the router, the administrator can verify the IP address configuration using either the telnet or ping command.

Configuring RIP

Routing Information Protocol (RIP) is a category of distance-vector routing protocol that employs the hop-count routing metric to choose a route. In an RIP network, the maximum hop count is 15. The 16th hop is infinity.

To configure a RIP router, the following commands must be executed from the global configuration mode:

```
router rip
```

```
network <network-number>
```

where:

- *router rip*: Defines RIP as the protocol
- *network number*: Denotes the IP address of the directly linked network

For example:

```
router rip
```

```
network 5.0.0.0
```

RIP information can be viewed by using the following commands:

- *show ip route*: Displays and checks IP routes in the routing table of a router, revealing all IP routes that are connected statically or directly to the local router

- *show ip protocol*: Displays and checks information such as the protocol used, routing timers, and other information linked with the local router

IP Source Routing

IP source routing allows the user to take control over the routing information present in the routing table of a router by specifying the route taken by an IP datagram to reach its destination. The router uses this information and skips all the alternate methods needed to reach the remote host. An attacker can take advantage of IP source routing to carry out IP spoofing attacks on a router. Because of this vulnerability, this feature is often disabled on a router.

Configuration Sources

Routers can be configured using external or internal sources. In order to configure the files, the user has to logon in global configuration mode. To quickly connect the router to the network, it is recommended to use the setup configuration mode. There are two choices to select from for this mode: basic management or extended setup.

CLI mode is used to manually configure a router. The CLI configuration modes are classified into three types: user EXEC, privileged EXEC, and global configuration. Various commands are used to view and manipulate the routing information.

External Configuration Sources

External configuration uses external sources to configure a router. The types of external configuration sources include the following:

- *Console port*: This is a port on the router that is typically used for the initial configuration.
- *Auxiliary port*: This asynchronous port is configured as data terminal equipment (DTE) to configure and control a router. A dial-up modem is attached to the auxiliary port to use asynchronous remote dial-up access, along with a terminal emulator to configure the router.
- *Virtual terminals*: Five virtual terminals, numbered 0–4, allows an administrator to maintain and configure the router. When the initial configuration of the router is set, the terminals are configured to manage the router via telnet.
- *TFTP server*: A TFTP server is used to download configuration files from and upload configuration files to the router.

Internal Configuration Sources

Internal configurations sources within the router include the following:

- *Random access memory (RAM)/Dynamic random access memory (DRAM)*: RAM stores the router's dynamic configuration information until the router is switched off.
- *Nonvolatile random access memory (NVRAM)*: This contains a backup copy of the configuration file. When the router is starting, it boots from NVRAM.
- *Flash memory*: This contains Cisco IOS and other IOSs. When the power is switched off, the contents of flash memory are not lost.
- *Read-only memory (ROM)*: This contains the bootstrap program that boots the router. It uses a small monitoring system to recover the router when it is down.

Router Initiation

When a router starts up, it goes through the following steps:

1. *Power-on self-test (POST)*: When the router is switched on, it checks the hardware, diagnoses all the modules, and verifies the basic operations of the CPU, memory, and interfaces.
2. *Loading Cisco IOS*: After POST, the router loads the Cisco IOS.
3. *Applying router configuration information*: After loading IOS, the router searches for the configuration file. If no configuration file is found, it enters setup mode to set up the new configuration settings for the router.

Loading the Configuration Files

In order to configure the files, the user has to logon in global configuration mode. Configuration files can be copied using the following commands:

- *copy tftp running-config*: Copies the configuration files to RAM from the TFTP server
- *copy tftp startup-config*: Copies the configuration files to NVRAM from the TFTP server
- *copy startup-config running-config*: Copies the configuration files to RAM from NVRAM, deleting all existing data

Configuring from a TFTP Server

A TFTP server keeps a backup of all the configuration files. Workstations can operate as TFTP servers and can download files from routers. To configure a router from a TFTP server, an administrator first copies the configuration files to RAM from the TFTP server.

A prompt will ask for the type of configuration file (host or network). The host configuration file consists of the commands that relate to a specific router, while the network configuration file contains commands that are employed to every network router. The host file is the default configuration file.

When prompted for the IP address, the administrator provides the address of the remote host that is the source of the configuration file. Then, he or she provides a name for the configuration file when the application prompts to be stored on the TFTP server.

Setup Configuration Mode

To quickly connect the router to the network, an administrator can use the setup configuration mode. This can be done in either basic management or extended setup mode. The router can be accessed from anywhere in the network if it is configured in basic management mode, but it needs to be in extended setup mode to be configured and managed.

When configuring the router in extended setup mode, the following dialog appears:

```
---System Configuration Dialog ---

At any point, enter a question mark '?' for help.

Use ctrl-c to abort configuration dialog at any prompt.

The Default settings are in square brackets '[]'.

Would you like to enter the initial configuration dialog?

[yes/no]: y

Would you like to enter basic management setup?

[yes/no]: n

First, would you like to see the current interface summary?

[yes]: return

Any interface listed with OK? value "NO" does not have a valid
configuration

Interface IP-Address OK? Method Status Protocol

ATM1/0 unassigned NO unset down down

FastEthernet2/0 unassigned NO unset down down
```

The above step presents the user with an idea of various router interfaces. Before the router starts sending data packets across the network, all of its interfaces should be configured.

Setting up Passwords and Configuring Routing Protocols

The following are the steps for setting up passwords:

1. First, create a hostname for the router.

2. Next, create an enable secret password. This is a one-way cryptographic secret password that can be used instead of the enable password.

3. Next, create an enable password. The enable password is used when there is no enable secret password and when using older software and some boot images.

The enable secret and enable password parameters require distinct values. If the values match, the following warning is displayed:

```
%Please choose a password that is different from the enable secret.
```

The enable secret is an encrypted password that overrides the enable password.

Not specifying an enable password allows the user to switch to the privileged EXEC mode without the need for a password. This could allow an attacker to easily change the configuration of a router if he or she gains access to the router's interface. Security to the router's interface is provided through the virtual terminal password.

The following shows a transcript of the questions asked about configuring routing protocols:

```
Enter virtual terminal password: connect

Configure SNMP Network Management? [yes]:

Community string [public]:

Configure Vines? [no]:

Configure LAT? [no]:

Configure AppleTalk? [no]:

Multizone networks? [no]:

Configure DECnet? [no]:

Configure IP? [yes]:

Configure IGRP routing? [yes]:

Your IGRP autonomous system number [1]: 15

Configure RIP routing? [no]:

Configure CLNS? [no]: n

Configure bridging? [no]:

Configure IPX? [no]:

Configure XNS? [no]:

Configure Apollo? [no]:
```

Then, the system prompts for router interface configuration.

Interface Configuration

```
Configuring interface parameters:

Configuring interface ATM1/0:

Is this interface in use? [yes]:

Configure IP on this interface? [yes]:

IP address for this interface: 1.1.1.10

Number of bits in subnet field [0]:

Class C network is 1.1.1.0, 0 subnet bits; mask is /24

Configuring interface FastEthernet2/0:
```

```
Is this interface in use? [yes]:

Use the 100 Base-TX (RJ-45) connector? [yes]:

Operate in full-duplex mode? [no]:

Configure IP on this interface? [yes]:

IP address for this interface: 1.1.1.20

Number of bits in subnet field [0]:

Class C network is 1.1.1.0, 0 subnet bits; mask is /24
```

The steps to configure the interface of the router vary from hardware to hardware. After the configuration is complete, the user is prompted to accept, modify, or reject the final configuration.

CLI Configuration Mode

CLI mode is used to manually configure a router. The CLI configuration modes are classified into three types: user EXEC, privileged EXEC, and global configuration.

User EXEC Mode

After the initial router configuration in setup mode, the administrator can enter user EXEC mode. The user EXEC command prompt consists of the router name followed by the > symbol.

In this mode, the configuration of a router cannot be changed. Commands are used to show the current configuration and run utilities like ping, telnet, and traceroute, as well as to troubleshoot network connectivity. The command set and their functions are displayed when the user types **?** at the command prompt. Table 2-1 shows some of the available commands in user EXEC mode.

Privileged EXEC Mode

This mode helps the administrator debug and test the router configuration, modify configuration files, and access different modes of configuration. The enable command allows the administrator to enter privileged EXEC mode from user EXEC mode.

To view the command list available in this mode, the administrator can type **?** at the command prompt. Table 2-2 shows the commands of privileged EXEC mode.

Global Configuration Mode

In this mode, a router is configured manually. Global configuration commands apply to features that affect the whole system.

An administrator uses the configure command in privileged EXEC mode to enter this mode. This mode is divided into a number of submodes that allow the administrator to configure specific features on a router. For example, to configure an interface, he or she enters the router interface configuration submode.

Once finished with this mode, the administrator can use Ctrl+Z, the end command, or the exit command to exit the mode and return to the privileged prompt. Table 2-3 shows the commands in global configuration mode.

Interface Configuration Mode

Interface configuration mode allows an administrator to modify the operation of interfaces. Features are enabled according to the current interface.

Line Configuration Mode

Line configuration mode is used to configure CLI access to the router. To login to this mode from the configuration prompt, the administrator can use the line command followed by the line type—such as vty, console, or tty—and a line number. To exit line configuration mode and return to EXEC mode, the administrator can use **Ctrl+Z** or the end command.

ROM Monitor Mode

The ROM monitor mode starts when the router boots up and cannot find a valid system image. This mode is needed when the system boot parameters are changed and the system password is reset. When the router has a working image installed on it, an administrator can press the break key in the first 60 seconds of the router boot sequence to initiate this mode. The ROM monitor mode is used to perform low-level diagnostics, recover from system failure, and stop the boot process.

Command	Function
access-enable	Create a temporary access-list entry
access-profile	Apply user profile to interface
clear	Reset functions
connect	Open a terminal connection
disable	Turn off privileged commands
disconnect	Disconnect an existing network connection
enable	Turn on privileged commands
exit	Exit from the EXEC
help	Description of the interactive help system
lock	Lock the terminal
login	Log in as a particular user
logout	Exit from the EXEC
mrinfo	Request neighbor and version information from a multicast router
mstat	Show statistics after multiple multicast traceroute
mtrace	Trace reverse multicast path from destination to source
name-connection	Name an existing network connection
pad	Open an X.29 PAD connection
ping	Send echo messages
ppp	Start IETF point-to-point protocol (PPP)
resume	Resume an active network connection
rlogin	Open an rlogin connection
show	Show running system information
slip	Start serial-line IP (SLIP)
systat	Display information about terminal
terminal	Open a telnet connection
traceroute	Trace route to destination
tunnel	Open a tunnel connection
where	List active connections
x28	Become an X.28 PAD

Table 2-1 These are the commands available in user EXEC mode

Command	Function
access-enable	Create a temporary access-list entry
access-template	Create a temporary access-list entry
bfe	For manual emergency modes setting
clear	Reset functions
clock	Manage the system clock
configure	Enter configuration mode
connect	Open a terminal connection
copy	Copy configuration or image data
debug	Debugging functions
disable	Turn off privileged commands
disconnect	Disconnect an existing network connection
enable	Turn on privileged commands
erase	Erase flash or configuration memory
exit	Exit from the EXEC
help	Describe the interactive help system
lock	Lock the terminal
login	Log in as a particular user
logout	Exit from the EXEC
mrinfo	Request neighbor and version information from multicast router
mstat	Show statistics after multiple multicast traceroutes
mtrace	Trace reverse multicast path from destination to source
name-connection	Name an existing network connection
no	Disable debugging functions
pad	Open a X.29 PAD connection
ping	Send echo messages
ppp	Start IETF point-to-point protocol (PPP)
reload	Halt and perform a cold restart
resume	Resume an active network connection
rlogin	Open an rlogin connection
rsh	Execute a remote command
send	Send a message to other TTY lines
setup	Run the setup command facility
show	Show running system information
systat	Display information about terminal lines
terminal	Set terminal line parameters
test	Test subsystems, memory, and interfaces
traceroute	Trace route to destination
tunnel	Open a tunnel connection
undebug	Disable debugging functions
verify	Verify checksum of a flash file
where	List active connections
write	Write running configuration to memory, network, or terminal
x28	Become an X.28 PAD
x3	Set X.3 parameters on PAD

Table 2-2   These are the commands available in privileged EXEC mode

Command	Function
aaa	Authentication, authorization, and accounting
access-list	Add an access-list entry
alias	Create command alias
appletalk	Appletalk global configuration commands
arap	Appletalk remote access protocol
airp	Set a static ARP entry
async-bootp	Modify system BOOTP parameters
autonomous-system	Specify local AS number
banner	Define a login banner
boot	Modify system boot parameters
bridge	Bridge group
buffers	Adjust system buffer pool parameters
busy-message	Display message when connection to host fails
call-history-mib	Define call history MIB parameters
cdp	Global CDP configuration commands
chat-script	Define a modem chat script
config-register	Define the configuration register
clock	Configure time-of-day clock
decnet	Global DECnet configuration subcommands
default	Set a command to its defaults
default-value	Default character-bits values
dialer-list	Create a dialer-list entry
dnsix-dmdp	Provide DMDP service for DNSIX
dnsix-nat	Provide DNSIX service for audit trails
downward-compatible-config	Create a configuration compatible with older software
enable	Modify enable password parameters
end	Exit from configure mode
exception	Exception handling
exit	Exit from configure mode
frame-relay	Global frame relay configuration commands
help	Display the interactive help system
hostname	Set system's network name
interface	Select an interface to configure
ip	Global IP configuration subcommands
ipx	Novell/IPX global configuration commands
key	Key management
line	Configure a terminal line
logging	Modify message logging facilities
login-string	Define a host-specific login string
map-class	Configure a static map class
map-list	Configure a static map list
menu	Define a user-interface menu
modemcap	Modem capabilities database
mop	Configure the DEC MOP server
multilink	PPP multilink global configuration
netbios	NetBIOS access control filtering

Table 2-3 These are the commands in global configuration mode *(continues)*

Command	Function
no	Negate a command or set its defaults
ntp	Configure NTP
partition	Partition device
printer	Define an LPD printer
priority-list	Build a priority list
privilege	Command privilege parameters
prompt	Set system's prompt
queue-list	Build a custom queue list
resume-string	Define a host-specific resume string
rif	Source-route RIF cache
rlogin	Rlogin configuration commands
rmon	Remote monitoring
route-map	Create route map or enter route-map command mode
router	Enable a routing process
scheduler	Scheduler parameters
service	Modify use of network-based services
smrp	Simple multicast routing protocol (SMRP) commands
snmp-server	Modify SNMP parameters
state-machine	Define a TCP dispatch state machine
tacacs-server	Modify TACACS query parameters
terminal-queue	Terminal queue commands
tftp-server	Provide TFTP service for netload requests
username	Establish username authentication
virtual-profile	Dialer global configuration
x25	X.25 level 3
x29	X.29 commands

Table 2-3   **These are the commands in global configuration mode** (*continued*)

Understanding TCP and UDP Small Servers and Various Tools

Finger Tool

This UNIX service provides information about the users logged on to a computer. Implementations of the finger service are also available for Windows platforms. The finger service is activated by default on a router, so it is important to disable this service on a Cisco router.

For example, take the following output of the finger service:

```
Line User Host(s) Idle Location

110 vty 2 192.16.14.02 00:15:00 192.15.14.01

112 vty 1 192.16.14.02 00:25:00 192.14.10.02

0 con 0 idle 05:00:00
```

This indicates that two end users are logged on to the router using effective terminals and one end user is logged on through the front-end port. It also provides information about the length of the session and the location of each end user. The **no service finger** command can be used in the universal configuration mode to disable the finger service.

Disabling the Auxiliary Port

The auxiliary port permits the user to alter the router configuration by remotely connecting to the router. The auxiliary port must be used to configure the router only if the user cannot connect using the front-end workstation or the telnet service. The **no exec** command deactivates the auxiliary port on a router.

Closing Extra Interfaces

A router has a variety of LAN and WAN interfaces. To minimize points of contact that can be exploited by attackers, all unused interfaces must be shut down. The shutdown command closes a router interface until it is necessary. The **no shutdown** command must be used in the interface configuration submode to make the interface active again.

BOOTP Service

The Bootstrap Protocol (BOOTP) service allows a router to acquire configuration details at startup from a BOOTP server. This service is activated by default on every router. Even though it helps simplify the boot process, it is often deactivated to increase security. It can be easy for an attacker to load a spoofed configuration on a router from a BOOTP server and hijack the network traffic. The **no ip bootp server** command deactivates the BOOTP service on a router.

TCP and UDP Small Servers

These services are also known as minor services. They assist in troubleshooting network connectivity among the diverse hosts on a network. Although these services are helpful as analytical tools, they should be disabled to prevent an attacker from using them for any one of several attacks, including TCP or UDP floods. To disable TCP small servers, an administrator can use the **no service tcp-small-servers** command. To disable UDP small servers, he or she can use the **no service udp-small-servers** command. These services are disabled by default on Cisco IOS version 11.3 and higher. They can be enabled using the **service tcp-small-servers** and **service udp-small-servers** commands.

Proxy ARP

Address Resolution Protocol (ARP) converts the network addresses of workstations on a LAN segment into MAC addresses. This service is activated by default on all IP interfaces of Cisco routers. The **no ip proxy-arp** command is used in the interface configuration mode to halt this service.

SNMP

Simple Network Management Protocol (SNMP) allows users to manage network devices from any location on the network. SNMP server is activated by default on Cisco routers. SNMP should be deactivated, though, because SNMP versions 1 and 2 do not guarantee trusted transmissions. The **no snmp-server** command is used in the universal configuration mode to deactivate SNMP. SNMP version 3 has significantly higher security than the previous versions and can be used to administer a router, if necessary.

NTP

Cisco IOS supports Network Time Protocol (NTP), which can be used to coordinate the time settings for network devices. The administrator can either disable NTP on a router or use ACLs to facilitate NTP reviews only from internal time servers. Earlier versions of Cisco IOS use the **no ntp enable** command to disable this feature, though current versions use the **ntp disable** command.

Hardening Routers

The main gateway between the network and the Internet is the router, so it is vulnerable to attacks from both inside and outside the network. It must be manually configured to minimize these attacks.

Display Notifications on Banners

Banners are used to display warnings to the user logging onto the router. These banners are configured in the global configuration mode. This does not ensure security but allows an administrator to attempt to prevent access to restricted areas. To configure a warning banner, the administrator uses the **banner motd** command and enters the banner.

Securing Terminal Sessions

Cisco IOS permits the router to provide sessions using various line terminals, such as console and virtual line terminals. Utilities like telnet and HyperTerminal are used to establish these sessions. By providing security measures like user authentication and session timeout periods, these sessions attempt to keep unauthorized users from accessing the router.

Passwords and Secrets

Passwords make sure that only authorized users can access the router. Cisco IOS provides two types of passwords: enable and line. Enable passwords control access to the privileged EXEC configuration mode. Line passwords help end users authenticate after logging in. The end user must be in global configuration mode to configure line passwords.

Console Password

Console passwords are used to modify the router configuration. The **line console 0** command sets a console password, which will grant only authorized users access to the router from the console terminal.

Virtual Terminal Password

This password helps authenticate telnet sessions initiated by remote end users. The **line vty 0** command helps to configure a virtual terminal password. By default, a virtual terminal password should be configured to authenticate telnet sessions. If a password is not set, the router refuses connection requests and sends an error message. The error message indicates that the connection is not completed because the virtual terminal password is not configured on that router. The **no login** command in the global configuration mode configures the router to accept a telnet connection without a password.

Auxiliary Password

Auxiliary passwords are used to authenticate a session set up using the auxiliary port of the router. The **line aux** command is used to configure an auxiliary password.

Encrypting Passwords

Router passwords must be protected against attacks. The **service password-encryption** command encrypts every password stored on the router.

Creating End User Accounts

Creating user accounts allows the administrator to set privileges for different users. The username command permits the administrator to generate an end user account on a router, as follows:

```
username njordan password admin1

username njordan privilege level 1
```

The **login local** command indicates that both a username and password must be specified when using a line terminal to establish a connection with the router. The **login** command requires only a password to establish a connection with the router. To delete an end-user account, the administrator can append the word "no" before the username command, as follows:

```
no username njordan
```

Privilege Levels

IOS software provides 16 different privilege levels, numbered from 0 to 15. Privilege level 0 contains a few command options that permit users to view a limited amount of router information. Privilege level 1 corresponds to the user EXEC mode, which provides a limited command set. Privilege level 15 contains the full set of CLI-mode configuration commands. Modifications in configuring a router are mostly done at privilege level 15, corresponding to the privileged EXEC mode. The router configuration commands are associated with higher privilege levels and the basic commands with lower privilege levels. The following commands show how to move some CLI commands from privilege level 1 to privilege level 15:

```
privilege exec level 15 telnet

privilege exec level 15 show running-config

privilege exec level 15 show interfaces
```

```
privilege exec level 15 show terminal

privilege exec level 1 show
```

The above code moves the telnet, **show running-config, show interfaces,** and **show terminal** commands to the privileged EXEC mode. Thus, these commands cannot be run from the end-user EXEC mode. The last configuration command moves the show command back to privilege level 1.

Session Timeout Periods

Session timeout values must be defined for all types of connections on a router in order to guarantee that each session is closed after a reasonable time period. This prevents an attacker from taking over a session. The **exec-timeout** command defines the value for the session timeout period, as follows:

```
exec-timeout 10 30
```

The first number denotes the minutes, while the second number denotes the seconds.

Cisco Discovery Protocol (CDP)

The Cisco Discovery Protocol (CDP) is used to trace the addresses of neighboring devices and to discover the platform of those devices. CDP can also show the interfaces a router is using. CDP is independent of the media and protocol, and is used mainly to discover the topology.

CDP works with SNMP, using a set of MIBs known as CISCO-CDP-MIB. CDP runs on layer 2 by using the Sub-Network Access Protocol (SNAP), which is based on configurable timers. CDP devices send timely updates to the multicast address. This timely update has a time-to-live field. The information in CDP is based on the user requests.

The **show cdp neighbors** command gives information about every CDP-enabled neighbor that is connected, including the following:

- *Device ID*: Device name on the network
- *Local interface*: The port of the device that is connected
- *Hold time*: For how much time the information is valid
- *Capability*: Reported as a code for router, switch, IGMP, bridge, or host
- *Port ID*: The port of the remote device

The **show cdp neighbors detail** command provides the following additional information:

- IP address of the remote interface
- Duplex setting
- CDP version in use
- Software version running on the device

Configuring CDP

Enabling and Disabling CDP on Cisco Devices CDP is enabled on Cisco routers by default. To disable CDP, an administrator uses the **no cdp run** command. To start CDP, an administrator uses the **cdp run** command in the global configuration mode.

Enabling and Disabling CDP on an Interface When CDP is run globally by the **cdp run** command, it is enabled by default on all supported interfaces (ports). CDP can be disabled on an interface that supports CDP (in this case, interface s1) using the **no cdp enabled** command as follows:

```
configure terminal

interface s1

no cdp enable
```

Logging

Logging in the router allows the administrator to analyze the network as well as investigate any problems or attacks on the network. There are many logging applications available to track and record logs from the network. Many of these applications can direct the log messages to e-mail and cell phones.

Level	Title	Description
0	Emergency	System is unusable
1	Alert	Immediate action is needed
2	Critical	A critical condition has occurred
3	Error	An error condition has occurred
4	Warning	A warning condition has occurred
5	Notification	A noteworthy event
6	Information	Informative message
7	Debugging	Debugging message

Table 2-4   **Lower router log priority numbers indicate higher priority messages**

Log Priority

There is a built-in function in routers to prioritize log messages. The priority ranges from 0 to 7, with a lower number indicating a higher-priority message. Table 2-4 shows the log priorities.

Time-Stamping

Routers record the date and time events occur. The command to turn on time-stamping is **service timestamps log datetime localtime**.

Cisco Logging Options

Logging is done to collect as much useful information as possible, but in limited quantities. Too much information will complicate matters, making it difficult to act on real threats. The log files must be monitored regularly. Log analysis is performed in a highly secure area in real time, and the findings are then forwarded to e-mail or a cell phone.

Console Logging

Console logging messages are displayed on the console port, so the administrator must log on to the console port to view them. By default, the console is configured at level 5, which displays the messages of that notification level or above.

To view the logging messages, the administrator has to set the console level to 7. The **logging console** command changes the console logging level.

Disabling Console Logging

Some of the messages can be discarded by changing to a higher priority level or disabling logging to the console altogether, because the console log messages require CPU time. Router performance can be increased by disabling logging to the console port. Disabling console logging is done using the **no logging console** command.

Buffered Logging

Buffered logging stores copies of log messages in RAM. Because there is a limited size for the buffer, when new messages are added to the buffer, older messages get deleted. This keeps only recent messages in the buffer without filling the router's memory. The router's logging buffer size should be configured with respect to the size of the RAM. All logs in the buffer include a time stamp.

Terminal Logging

By default, log messages are not sent to the terminal session. To view logging on the console port, the **terminal monitor** command is used.

Syslog Logging

Cisco routers can send their log messages to a syslog server. This is considered the best method of logging, because all log messages are sent directly to the server, which stores them. When configure syslog logging on a Cisco router, the administrator should keep the following in mind:

- The destination host can be specified using a hostname, DNS name, or IP address.
- The syslog facility names go from local 0 to local 7.
- The source interface for the message is the actual interface through which the messages are sent to the syslog server.

Router Configuration Commands

Router configuration commands are used to configure many aspects of the router, including the following:

- Enable the routing interface configuration mode on the device
- Create VLAN or loopback routing interfaces
- Review the usability status of an interface configured for IP
- Set the IP addresses for the interface
- Enable the interface for IP routing at device startup

Commands used to review and configure the interface settings include the following:

- interface
- show interface
- show ip interface
- ip address
- ip proxy-arp
- ip redirects
- ip unreachable
- mac-address
- mtu
- host-mobility
- show ip host-mobility
- shutdown
- no shutdown

Interface

The **interface** command sets the router into interface configuration mode, which is used to configure the specified physical port, loopback interface, or VLAN. Its syntax is as follows:

```
interface {vlan.1.vlan-id | loopbackloopback-id | port-string}
```

This command configures interfaces for IP routing. It enters router interface configuration mode, and, if the interface has not previously been created, creates a new routing interface. VLANs must be created from the switch CLI before they can be configured for IP routing.

The **show interface** command displays interface information for a single interface or for all interfaces. Its syntax is as follows:

```
show interface [eth0 | port-string]
```

If a physical interface has not been configured as an IP-routed interface, the information displayed by this command is limited to physical port information.

Managing Router Configuration

The configuration of the router is done with the router-mode CLI commands, while switch configuration is done with switch-mode CLI commands. Router commands are used to review and save the current router configuration.

The **show running-config** command displays the user-supplied router configuration commands entered while configuring the router. Its syntax is as follows:

```
show running-config [section] [outfile path-to/outfilename] [| search
regexp]
```

The optional section parameter displays only the specified section of the configuration. A list of valid section names can be displayed by entering **show running-config ?**

The optional **outfile path-to/outfilename** parameter specifies the file in which to store the configuration. Options for path-to are a file path on the active or standby CM, a file path on a USB drive attached to the active or standby CM, or the URL of an FTP, SCP (secure copy), or TFTP server.

The **show startup-config** command displays the current router startup configuration. The **show startup-config** command is used as follows:

```
show startup-config [outfile path-to/outfilename] [| search regexp]
```

As with **show-running-config**, the optional **outfile path-to/outfilename** parameter specifies the file in which to store the configuration.

The write command saves the router running configuration. Its syntax is simply **write <file>.**

Access Control Lists (ACLs)

An access control list (ACL) includes a set of conditions along with permit and deny command statements. It filters out undesired network traffic. Improved network security is guaranteed by the application of ACLs at various locations in a network. The role of ACLs must be defined in the overall network security policy of an enterprise. Cisco IOS facilitates different types of ACLs to protect a router against security threats like DoS attacks and IP address spoofing.

The benefits of ACL include:

- Providing extra security measures including hardening the Cisco IOS
- Controlling the flow of data packets by IP address
- Blocking unwanted network traffic and allowing a limited number of end users to access network resources

Creating a Standard ACL

While configuring an ACL, an administrator should note the following points:

- A unique number or name must be given to distinguish each ACL.
- A single ACL is applicable to multiple router interfaces or virtual line terminals.
- A single inbound or outbound ACL is applied at a time to a particular router interface or virtual line terminal.
- A default entry is added as the last entry of an ACL. This entry blocks all traffic that doesn't match the specifications.
- Specific permit or deny conditions must be specified before the generic conditions in an ACL.

A standard ACL allows or denies traffic based on the source IP address in the data packet. Multiple ways to permit or deny entries must be established within a single ACL. To create a standard ACL, the administrator first enters global configuration mode and then uses the access-list command to display the various numbered ranges relating to ACLs as follows:

- 1–99: IP standard access list
- 100–199: IP extended access list
- 1000–1099: IPX SAP access list
- 1100–1199: Extended 48-bit MAC-address access list
- 1200–1299: IPX summary address access list

- 200–299: Protocol type-code access list
- 300–399: DECnet access list
- 600–699: Appletalk access list
- 700–799: 48-bit MAC-address access list
- 800–899: IPX standard access list
- 900–999: IPX extended access list

The numbered range 1–99 denotes IP standard access lists. The administrator can select a number within the range to configure an IP standard ACL. To assign a number to a standard ACL, the administrator can use the following commands:

```
access-list

access-list 50
```

Cisco IOS prompts the administrator to define permit or deny conditions for the ACL. After the administrator defines the permit or deny conditions, Cisco IOS prompts him or her to specify the source IP address for those conditions.

The administrator can repeat the steps to configure multiple entries depending on the security requirements. Cisco IOS assumes the implicit deny condition as the default last entry in the ACL.

Creating an Extended ACL

An extended ACL filters network traffic based on multiple parameters. To configure an extended ACL, the administrator enters global configuration mode and again uses the access-list command to display the numbered ranges of ACLs. The numbered range 100–199 corresponds to IP extended access lists. The administrator selects a number within the range to configure an IP extended ACL, as follows:

```
access-list

access-list 150
```

After defining a number to identify the extended ACL, the administrator defines the permit or deny conditions to sort network traffic. He or she can select the network protocol to be used for filtering data traffic. Next, the administrator specifies the source IP address and destination IP address to use in the filter. The administrator can also define specific port numbers to use in the filter.

Creating a Named ACL

An ACL defined with a unique alphanumeric name instead of a number is called a named ACL. The number of named ACLs is not limited to a specific range. Using named ACLs, it is possible to delete specific entries from an ACL without reconstructing the entire ACL.

To configure a named standard IP ACL, the administrator first enters the global configuration mode and then uses the **ip access-list** command to specify a name for the ACL, as follows:

```
ip access-list standard
```

Setting the permit or deny conditions for a named ACL is similar to the method for a numbered ACL.

Creating a Time-Based ACL

This type of ACL is an extension of extended ACLs. A time-based ACL describes a time range along with the permit or deny conditions in an ACL. The time-range command specifies the days of the week and the time period used in an ACL. The two methods to specify time range are:

- *Periodic*: Defines a time range using the names of the days in a week with time values
- *Absolute*: Defines a time range using beginning and end time dates

In the following example, the Range123 time range is established using a periodic time-range command. The periodic command is followed by the names of the days in a week and time values in hh:mm format:

```
time-range Range123

periodic Tuesday Friday 8:00 to 18:00
```

The administrator can then establish an extended ACL and associate the time range called Range123 with it. The extended ACL in the example allows FTP transfers between two hosts:

```
access-list 105 permit tcp host 175.10.13.2 192.16.14.2 eq ftp

access-list 105 permit tcp host 175.10.13.2 host 192.16.15.2 eq ftp time-
range Range123
```

Implementing an ACL

By connecting an ACL to a router interface or a virtual line terminal, the flow of traffic across a router can be controlled. The correct placement of ACLs guarantees proper flow of network traffic.

A standard IP ACL must be applied to the destination host, when possible, and an extended IP ACL must be applied to the source host. ACLs should be placed at the incoming interface of the router to block all network traffic, or they should be placed at the outgoing interface of the router to block selected network traffic.

Applying an ACL to a Router Interface

The **ip access-group** command is used to apply an ACL to a router interface. The following commands apply an inbound ACL to the Ethernet interface:

```
int e0

no shutdown

ip access-group 1 in
```

To apply a named ACL, the administrator can replace the number with the name of an ACL. He or she can replace the word "in" with the word "out" to apply the list as an outbound list.

The access-class command applies an ACL to a virtual line terminal on the router. The following command in line configuration mode filters connection requests from remote end users:

```
line vty 0 4

access-class 105 in
```

Enabling the Turbo ACL Feature

ACL processing uses a good amount of CPU time. The router matches each entry in an ACL, one entry at a time, which can increase network latency when the ACL consists of many entries. The Turbo ACL feature manages the CPU processing load and speeds up the processing of data packets. It also arranges all ACLs on a router into lookup tables, keeping track of matching requirements specified in the ACL.

When Turbo ACL is enabled, a router matches data packets against the lookup tables. A time period for matching the data packets against the lookup tables is also defined, which decreases the load on the CPU of the router and speeds up the processing of data packets. This feature is disabled by default on a Cisco router. An administrator can use the **access-list compiled** command in the global configuration mode to enable the Turbo ACL feature.

ACL Security

Information about ACL violations must be frequently monitored and examined to identify possible attacks on a router. An administrator can use the log parameter to maintain a record of the violations of ACLs, as follows:

```
ip access-list 125 deny ip 145.25.10.14 any log

ip access-list 125 deny tcp 145.25.10.14 host 10.1.2.1 log

ip access-list 125 permit ip any log
```

Blocking Private IP Addresses

Internet Network Information Center (InterNIC) has described three blocks of IP addresses for personal networks. Any of these IP addresses can be utilized without any constraints on a personal network. Because these are purely for internal traffic, packets containing these IP addresses should be obstructed at both inward and outward router interfaces using these commands:

```
access-list 104 deny ip 192.168.0.0 0.0.255.255 any log

access-list 104 deny ip 172.16.0.0 0.15.255.255 any log

access-list 104 deny ip 10.0.0.0 0.255.255.255 any log
```

The following commands block outgoing packets containing private IP addresses:

```
access-list 105 deny ip any 192.168.0.0 0.0.255.255 log

access-list 105 deny ip any 172.16.0.0 0.15.255.255 log

access-list 105 deny ip any 10.0.0.0 0.255.255.255 log
```

Preventing DoS Attacks

DoS attacks utilize the vulnerabilities of protocols and services to interrupt network traffic. It is difficult to obstruct the various kinds of DoS attacks while permitting legitimate network use. The application of ACLs at the gateway router decreases the possibility of DoS attacks.

Preventing Smurf Attacks

An attacker carries out a Smurf attack using data packets with the spoofed IP address of the target host as the source address. To prevent these attacks, the **no ip directed-broadcast** command must be run for all interfaces of all routers within a network.

Preventing DDoS Attacks

It is very difficult to block DDoS attacks because an attacker uses multiple hosts to launch the attack. It is not possible to block traffic originating from these hosts because some of them may even be situated on trusted networks. Methods used to secure a router from DDoS attacks include:

- Egress and ingress filtering
- Unicast reverse path forwarding (RPF)

Committed Access Rate (CAR)

Committed Access Rate (CAR) is a form of traffic monitoring. When the network traffic load goes beyond the router's processing ability, CAR permits it to operate at a decreased level of performance. CAR policies also avoid interruption of router services due to DoS and DDoS attacks.

CAR employs rate-limit policies to control the stream of traffic. When CAR is configured and implemented, the router ceases all transmissions that go beyond the specified rate limit.

Apart from rate limiters, IP precedence levels can be defined for inbound and outbound data packets. These levels separate network traffic into different quality-of-service (QoS) categories.

Advantages of rate limiting using CAR include:

- The user can describe a high rate for traffic transmitted or received on an interface.
- It can shield a network from DoS attacks by stopping an excessive number of packets.
- It permits the user to configure rate-limit policies using fields such as IP precedence, media access control (MAC) addresses, and ACLs.

CAR can only be used with IP traffic.

Secure Shell (SSH)

Remote router management causes some security issues. Telnet is used to set up remote connections with a router to create changes to its configuration, and telnet passwords are interchanged between the router and the remote host in simple text layout. Secure Shell (SSH) provides a more protected option. It uses tough encryption and verification, encrypting all data exchanged during the logon process between the router and remote hosts.

Data encryption guarantees that information is protected from IP sniffing attacks. Its client-server architecture permits remote SSH clients to access an SSH server.

SSH is available for several different platforms, including UNIX, Windows, and Solaris. Authentication methods supported by SSH include:

- Password
- RSA authentication
- Kerberos
- Smart cards
- Digital certificates

Configuring SSH

The SSH server must first be activated on a router and executed as the default program for virtual line terminals. First, the administrator specifies a hostname, as follows:

```
hostname DefaultRouter
```

The administrator then uses the **ip domain-name** command to specify a DNS domain for the router. The router automatically attaches the domain name to the end of the hostname. The following example command shows a domain being specified:

```
ip domain-name mydomain.com
```

Next, the administrator specifies an RSA key pair to use with SSH. When an RSA key pair is described, SSH verification is automatically activated on a router. The capacity of the key extends from 260 bits to 2,048 bits. Cisco suggests a least size of 1,024 bits for the RSA key pair. The key pair is defined as follows:

```
crypto key generate rsa 1024
```

Clients must be verified and accounts must be created to scrutinize remote link requests. The AAA security model or the **login local** command can be implemented to facilitate verification and creation of client accounts, like so:

```
aaa new-model

username admin 1 password logOn134
```

The SSH server must be activated and configured to process requests from SSH clients. The **ip ssh** command must be executed in universal configuration mode to describe the connection timeout value and the number of attempts permitted before the connection request is rejected.

The following is an example of configuring these SSH parameters:

```
ip ssh time-out 120

ip ssh authentication-retries 3
```

SSH transmission must be sustained for virtual line terminals. These terminals are designed to use telnet as the original program. The **transport input** command must be executed in line configuration mode to describe SSH as the default program as follows:

```
line vty 0 4

transport input SSH
```

Routing Protocols

Routing Information Protocol

Routing Information Protocol (RIP) maintains the router information within a self-contained network like a LAN. The gateway hosts send the routing table to the closest neighbor every 30 seconds with information about other hosts. RIP uses hop count to determine the network distance. The host uses the routing table information to determine the next host to which to route the packet.

RIP sets a limit on the number of hops allowed from the source to the destination. The maximum number of hops allowed in the path is 15. Many timers are used in RIP, including routing update timer, route timeout timer, and route flush timer. The RIP packet consists of the following nine fields:

1. Command (1 octet) indicates whether a packet is a request or a response.

2. Version number (1 octet) gives the version of RIP being used.

3. (2-octet zero field)

4. Address-family identifier (2 octets) specifies the type of address being used.

5. (2-octet zero field)

6. IP address (4 octets) specifies the IP address for the entry.

7. (4-octet zero field)

8. (4-octet zero field)

9. Metric (4 octets) indicates how many hops are being traversed up to the destination. The value is between 1 and 15 for reachable routes and 16 for unreachable routes.

Interior Gateway Routing Protocol (IGRP)

The goal of IGRP is to provide a robust protocol within an autonomous system. It is a distance-vector interior gateway protocol using a combination of metrics: internetwork delay, bandwidth, reliability, and load. IGRP provides stability features including hold downs, split horizons, and poison-reverse updates.

IGRP stores event variables containing timing intervals. The variables include an update timer, an invalid timer, a hold period, and a flush timer. The update timer specifies how frequently the routing update messages are sent. The default value for this variable is 90 seconds.

How long a router waits in the absence of the routing update messages is specified in the invalid timer. The hold-down period is specified in the hold-time period variable.

Enhanced Interior Gateway Routing Protocol (EIGRP)

Enhanced Interior Gateway Routing Protocol (EIGRP) is an interior gateway protocol compatible with many topologies and transmission media. There are many advantages to using EIGRP, including the following:

- Minimum utilization of network resources

- Only routing table changes are propagated

- Low turnaround time

Routers running EIGRP store all information about their neighbors and quickly adopt the changes and alternate routes. If there is no alternate route, then the EIGRP queries its neighbors for the discovery of alternate routes. The query is continued until an alternate route is found. EIGRP makes partial updates when the metric for the route changes.

Troubleshooting Routers

Troubleshooting Commands

Cisco routers provide the following CLI commands for network information:

- *Show*: The show command presents statistics of a router or its components, and also verifies the current status of controllers, interfaces, etc.

- *Ping* and *trace*: These commands check for the proper configuration and functionality of devices by either pinging the devices or tracing the route to the devices.

- *debug*: The debug command is used to isolate problems in the network related to network traffic and router status, such as information about a protocol and routing events. This command can change the configuration of the router. For example, to view statistics about IGRP routing transactions and events, the administrator can execute the command **debug ip igrp events [ip address]**.

Troubleshooting with Network Management Tools

Networking management tools are used to configure, monitor, and troubleshoot network devices. These tools include the following:

- *CiscoView*: This is a graphical user interface (GUI) for troubleshooting devices like switches and routers. It also determines the effect of a changed configuration on network devices.
- *VLAN Director*: This tool helps administrators configure and troubleshoot VLANs.
- *Internetwork Performance Monitor (IPM)*: IPM monitors devices on the network. It monitors latency and response time, and troubleshoots and analyzes network problems.
- *Traffic Director*: This tool filters packets across networks and checks the load statistics on various routes.
- *Network analyzers*: These help administrators capture and filter packets (frames at layer 2), and also analyze and troubleshoot network problems by examining the performance of the network.

Troubleshooting IP Connectivity in Routers

To troubleshoot IP connectivity in routers:

- Compare and check the physical links connected to each network device, ensuring no disruption is being caused by the physical lines.
- Check the routes (static, dynamic, and default) configured to send the data packets to the desired node.
- Examine looping and other routing protocol–related problems.
- Verify the configurations in the software of network devices.
- Verify and resolve route conflicts.

Troubleshooting PPP and Frame Relay

To troubleshoot a point-to-point link:

- Check the physical connections between the network devices.
- Check the configurations of the router.
- Use these commands to check the status and statistics:

```
show dialer command

debug dialer

debug ppp negotiation

debug ppp authentication
```

- Verify the usernames and passwords.

Troubleshooting X.25

To troubleshoot X.25:

- Check the physical connections between network devices.
- Check the configurations of the routers.
- Verify that the X.25 mapping command is implemented on the correct interface.
- Verify the configuration with the following command:

```
debug x.25 events
```

Troubleshooting ISDN

To troubleshoot an ISDN link:

- Check the physical connections between network devices.
- Verify the router configuration.
- Check whether the **dialer map** and dialer-list commands are executed properly with all keywords.
- Verify that the interface is not down.
- Verify that the dialer pool is configured correctly.

Components of Router Security

Router security guidelines describe actions to guarantee the physical security of the router, persons certified to access the router, the verification scheme for users, and the nature of services provided by the router. The National Security Agency (NSA) Router Security Configuration Guide comprises a checklist that assists in defining security guidelines. The following are some of the key aspects in the checklist:

- *Physical security*: This includes the requirement of networking employees certified to install and uninstall the router, positioning of the front-end workstation and other peripheral devices, and the presence of a recovery process when router services are interrupted.
- *Static configuration security*: This defines guidelines to modify the configuration of a router, create and alter passwords, generate user accounts, and define remote verification keys. It also includes the revival procedure to be followed if the configuration file is compromised.
- *Dynamic configuration security*: This defines guidelines to describe the services to be activated on a router, such as the type of routing protocol; the sustained routing services along with the end users authenticated to access them; and the process to set the time on the router.
- *Network service security*: This defines guidelines to sort network traffic using ACLs and other network security measures. It describes protocols and the pertinent port numbers used to sort traffic on different interfaces of the router. Network service security also describes the responsibility of an Internet service provider (ISP) in the execution of router security.
- *Compromise response*: This describes the methods to reestablish router services after an attack. It describes the disaster management team that must be informed when a security attack takes place. This team executes the revival procedures and gathers proof that assists in tracking the probable source of the attack.

Router Security Testing Tools

- *Security Administrator's Integrated Network Tool (SAINT)*: SAINT scrutinizes network services to recognize network vulnerabilities. It executes TCP and UDP scans to identify the services on the host. SAINT can classify vulnerabilities according to type, complexity level, or commonality. It also suggests preventive measures.
- *Cisco Secure Scanner*: The Cisco Secure Scanner verifies network devices, such as routers, switches, and servers, to detect security vulnerabilities. It logs all vulnerabilities detected, compares them to a database, and offers solutions. This scanner can also produce reports in different formats, such as bar graphs and pie charts. The Grid Browser sorts the verification results and displays only required sections.
- *Security Administrator Tool for Analyzing Networks (SATAN)*: SATAN executes TCP and UDP scans to recognize security vulnerabilities.
- *Router Audit Tool (RAT)*: RAT monitors Cisco IOS routers to assess the security measures configured on them. This tool supports Windows and UNIX platforms.
- *CyberCop ASaP*: CyberCop ASaP presents an Internet-dependent vulnerability identification service.

Chapter Summary

- In packet-switched networks such as the Internet, a router is a piece of hardware or software that determines the next network point to which a packet should be forwarded.

- The three main types of routing algorithms are distance-vector algorithms, link-state algorithms, and hybrid algorithms.

- Cisco IOS is designed for the configuration of Cisco network devices, such as routers and switches.

- Routing Information Protocol (RIP) is a category of distance-vector routing protocol that employs the hop-count routing metric to choose a route.

- IOS software provides 16 different privilege levels, numbered from 0 to 15.

- An access control list (ACL) includes a set of conditions along with permit and deny command statements. It filters out undesired network traffic.

Review Questions

1. What are the router metrics in use?

2. What are link-state algorithms?

3. What is IOS?

4. Explain the ARP process.

5. What is IP routing?

6. What is IP source routing?

7. What is BOOTP?

8. Explain how to disable proxy ARP.

9. What is an auxiliary password?

10. Explain the process of encrypting passwords.

11. How is logging turned on?

12. Explain how to create a standard ACL.

Hands-On Projects

1. Read about routing basics.

   - Navigate to Chapter 2 of the Student Resource Center.
   - Open routing.pdf and read the content.

2. Read about hardening Cisco routers.

   - Navigate to Chapter 2 of the Student Resource Center.
   - Open Hardening Cisco Routers.pdf and read the content.

3. Read about router security configuration.

   - Navigate to Chapter 2 of the Student Resource Center.
   - Open router-security-configuration-guide.pdf and read the content.

4. Read about routing principles.

   - Navigate to Chapter 2 of the Student Resource Center.
   - Open Routing Principles.pdf and read the content.

5. Read about Routing Information Protocol (RIP).

   - Navigate to Chapter 2 of the Student Resource Center.
   - Open rip.pdf and read the content.

6. Read about troubleshooting routers.

   - Navigate to Chapter 2 of the Student Resource Center.
   - Open Troubleshooting Routers.pdf and read the content.

Chapter 3

Hardening Operating Systems

Objectives

After completing this chapter, you should be able to:

- Configure Windows
- Manage resources
- Understand Kerberos authentication and domain security
- Understand infrastructure, authentication, and auditing of Windows 2003
- Understand Windows certification authorities
- Secure Linux
- Configure Pluggable Authentication Modules (PAMs)
- Secure UNIX
- Secure Macintosh OS
- Install Windows Vista

Key Terms

Process   a program running on an operating system

Introduction to Hardening Operating Systems

A computer's operating system is its most fundamental, and complex, piece of software. It controls every other piece of software, and as such, it is critical that the operating system be secure. This chapter familiarizes you with how different operating systems handle security and how that security can be increased.

Configuring Windows

BIOS Security

There are a few steps that should be taken to secure the system's BIOS (basic input/output system), namely:

1. Update the BIOS.

2. Password-protect the BIOS configuration.

3. Prevent startup from removable media. It becomes much easier to hijack a system when the attacker can boot from removable media such as a CD-ROM, floppy disk, or USB drive.

Windows Registry

The registry is a centralized storage area in Windows, containing details of system configuration, devices, applications, user accounts, and ports. The information is stored in a sequential order with a specific hierarchy.

Editing the Registry

Windows tools such as Regedit.exe and Regedt32.exe can be used to edit the registry. This is a delicate task, because if the wrong information is deleted or changed, the entire operating system may need to be reinstalled. To prevent reinstalling, a registry backup must be maintained.

A registry editor displays the predefined keys in a folder. Keys such as HKEY_USERS and HKEY_LOCAL_MACHINE are used to configure computers. A key can be up to 255 characters long.

Table 3-1 shows some of the predefined keys used by the system.

Folder/Predefined Key	Description
HKEY_CURRENT_USER	This contains configuration information for the user currently logged on. The user's folders, screen colors, and Control Panel settings are stored here. This information is associated with the user's profile. This key is sometimes abbreviated as "HKCU."
HKEY_USERS	This contains all the actively loaded user profiles on the computer. HKEY_CURRENT_USER is a subkey of HKEY_USERS. It is sometimes abbreviated as "HKU."
HKEY_LOCAL_MACHINE	This contains configuration information particular to the computer, but not specific to any user. This key is sometimes abbreviated as "HKLM."
HKEY_CLASSES_ROOT	This is a subkey of HKEY_LOCAL_MACHINE\Software\Classes. The information stored here makes sure that the correct program opens when a file is opened using Windows Explorer. This key is sometimes abbreviated as "HKCR." Starting with Windows 2000, this information is stored under both the HKEY_LOCAL_MACHINE and HKEY_CURRENT_USER keys. The HKEY_LOCAL_MACHINE\Software\Classes key contains default settings that apply to all users on the local computer, while the HKEY_LOCAL_MACHINE\Software\Classes key contains settings that override the default settings and apply only to the current user. The HKEY_CLASSES_ROOT key provides a view of the registry that merges the information from these two sources. HKEY_CLASSES_ROOT also provides this merged view for programs designed for earlier versions of Windows. If changes are made to HKEY_CLASSES_ROOT, the system stores the information under HKEY_LOCAL_MACHINE\Software\Classes. However, if the key already exists under HKEY_CURRENT_USER Software Classes, the system will store the information there instead.
HKEY_CURRENT_CONFIG	This contains information about the hardware profile used by the local computer at system startup.

Table 3-1   These are some of the predefined Windows registry keys

Tool: RootkitRevealer

RootkitRevealer is an advanced rootkit detection utility. There are several different types of rootkits, including:

- *Persistent rootkits*: Persistent rootkits are associated with malware and activate each time the system boots. The code must be stored in a persistent store such as the registry or the file system in order to execute without any intervention.

- *Memory-based rootkits*: Memory-based rootkits have no persistent code and cannot survive a reboot.

- *User-mode rootkits*: A user-mode rootkit can intercept all the calls to Windows such as the findfirst-file and findnextfile APIs, which are used for file exploration utilities such as Explorer and the command prompt.

- *Kernel-mode rootkits*: Kernel-mode rootkits can intercept active APIs in kernel mode and can directly manipulate kernel data structures. The general technique for hiding the presence of malware is to remove the process from the kernel's active processes.

Manual Scanning

To scan systems, an administrator can launch RootkitRevealer and press the **Scan** button. The program will then scan the system, reporting its actions in a status area at the bottom of its window and noting any problems in the output list, as shown in Figure 3-1.

The **Hide NTFS Metadata Files** option is on by default, so it will not show standard NTFS metadata files that are hidden from the Windows API. The **Scan Registry option** is also on by default.

Automatic Scanning

RootkitRevealer supports several options for automatically scanning systems. Automatic scanning has the following options:

- *-a*: Automatically scan and exit when done
- *-c*: Format output as CSV
- *-m*: Show NTFS metadata files
- *-r*: Do not scan the registry

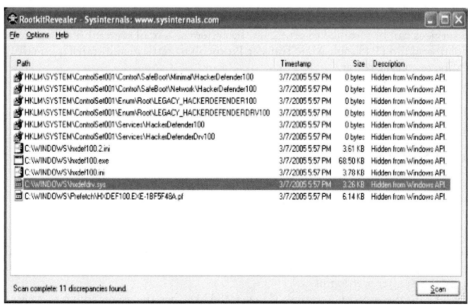

Source: http://technet.microsoft.com/en-us/sysinternals/bb897445.aspx. Accessed 2004.

Figure 3-1   RootkitRevealer will note any problems it finds as it finds them.

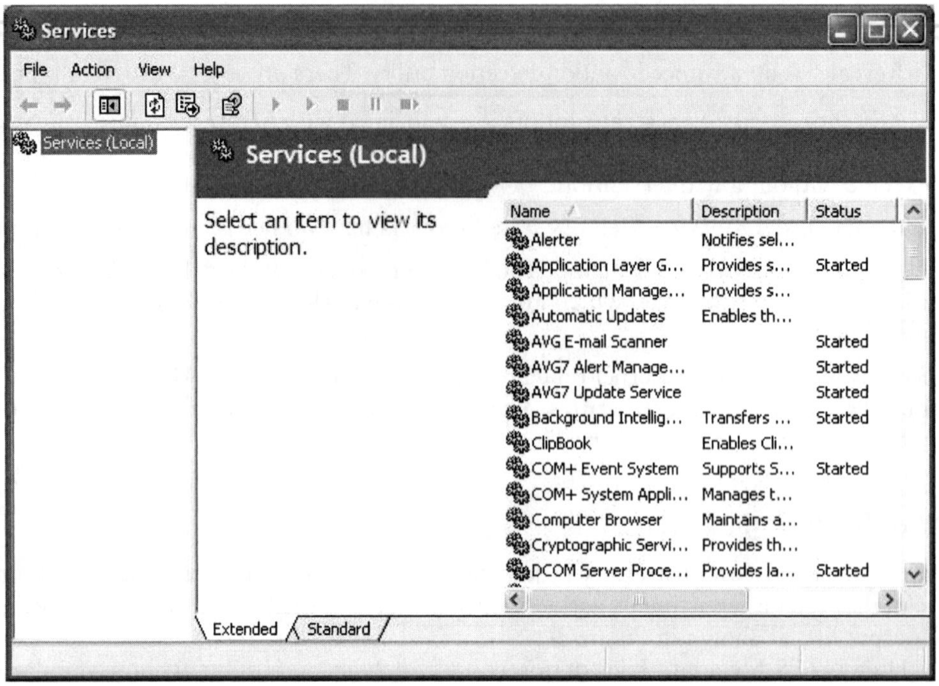

Figure 3-2 The service configuration tool is in the Control Panel's administrative tools.

Windows Services

Windows services are applications that automatically start and run in the background. To see a list of services and modify them, from the Windows Control Panel, an administrator can open **Administrative Tools** and then open **Services**. The service configuration tool shown in Figure 3-2 will appear.

Services can be modified using this tool. They can be manually started and stopped, or they can be configured to start automatically.

E-Mail Services

E-mail services can be installed to configure the system as a mail server. E-mail services use POP3 (Post Office Protocol 3) and SMTP (Simple Mail Transfer Protocol) to retrieve and transfer e-mails. The administrator creates mailboxes on the server.

The POP3 service is used by the administrator to manage and store mail accounts. It allows the user to connect to the mail server and retrieve e-mail on the local computer. SMTP, on the other hand, controls how the e-mail is transported and delivered. This service is automatically installed on a system where the POP3 service is running. SMTP allows the user to send outbound mail.

Regional Settings

Regional settings in Web servers apply to users of the site. They include functions such as how numbers and dates are displayed, how data is sorted, and time zones.

Logon Processes

Programs running on an operating system are known as *processes*. All local users and user groups are handled by the WinLogon process. This process transmits the user credentials for authentication to the Local Security Authority (LSA) after user logins.

The LSA calls the Security Accounts Manager (SAM) when the user is trying to access the system using a local account. SAM is a Windows operating system element that monitors the local account information database in the registry using the New Technology LAN Manager (NTLM) protocol. SAM matches the user information to the information stored in the database known as the Discretionary Access Control List (DACL), and if a proper match is found, the user is granted system access through the WinLogon process.

LSA calls the NetLogon process if the user is using a domain account. The NetLogon process runs within the domain controller. It receives the user information from LSA for authentication. If the user is authentic, NetLogon then creates an access token and returns authenticated logon information to WinLogon.

When the user accesses other systems of the same domain, the LSA transfers the access token and credentials from the local system to the LSA of other remote computers. In order to gain access to the remote system, the credentials sent must be authentic and trusted by the LSA of the other system. During remote system logon, the username and the password must be verified. If the user's credentials match, the authentication process is called transparent background authentication; otherwise, it again asks for the credentials from the local machine.

Security Identifiers (SIDs)

Security identifiers are used to authenticate different user accounts of a domain. These are unique serial numbers used to identify and authenticate system users. Security identifiers are assigned to individual users and group users, and are generated during account creation. SIDs are associated with each active account and used for user authentication each time the user logs on to the system.

Managing Resources

Windows provides access to resources through Windows Explorer and Directory Services Agent (DSA). The shell script in Windows initiates programs in user mode. When a new program is launched, Windows Explorer grants it an access token based on the user's access token, so every running program is associated with a user. The access token then allows access to system resources.

DSA is the service used to verify domain users with the help of the Local Security Authority and Active Directory. The WinLogon process starts from a user-generated interrupt: Ctrl+Alt+Del. A new access token is assigned to the user through the local Security Accounts Manager or the NetLogon service. Users call up the Directory Services Agent (DSA) on an Active Directory domain controller or the SAM on a Windows NT domain controller after getting an access token. The parent process is not involved in token generation.

Mandatory Logons

In Windows NT, it is mandatory to log on with a username and password. Even though a user can choose to automatically log in with credentials provided from the registry, the user account logon still exists.

Windows requires the Ctrl+Alt+Del keystroke to log in. The computer handles the Ctrl+Alt+Del keystroke as a hardware interrupt, so there is no way for a programmer to make the keystroke do something else. Without this feature, a hacker would be able to write a program that can display a fake login screen and collect passwords from unsuspecting users.

It is possible to set passwords to be blank. In this case, the user only needs to provide a username. The mandatory logon still occurs, but it is not secure without a password. This is the method used by default in Windows XP Home Edition. Users merely click an icon representing their identity and are not required to enter a password, unless they configure the operating system to ask for one.

Because the access token is passed to new programs when the programs are started, there is no further need to access the SAM database locally or Active Directory on a domain controller for authentication after the user has logged in.

Need-To-Know Controls

Well-defined authorization and access controls are essential to maintain need-to-know controls and privacy policies, as well as to protect sensitive information. The policy statements should provide clear guidance on the following:

- How to assign access privileges
- How to modify access privileges
- How to remove access privileges
- How to authorize access privilege
- How to audit access privileges

The policy must consider the following aspects:

- Sensitivity of the information
- Need-to-know considerations
- Privacy restrictions

Malicious Logic Protection

Malicious logic protection protects automated information systems (AISs) and networks from malicious logic attacks, including viruses, worms, Trojans, and bots.

The preventive measures to protect systems from malicious code or logic include:

- Using antivirus software and keeping it updated
- Scanning all incoming traffic
- Configuring antivirus software to scan inserted media immediately
- Preparing a report of all malicious logic attacks

Assurance

The controls needed for an acceptable level of system assurance are regulated by the Sarbanes-Oxley Act (SOX). The assurance level can be defined as the probability that the data contained in the system are accurate. While assessing the overall assurance of a system, auditors and management should think beyond the technical controls. The overall network and system infrastructure, as well as technical and administrative controls, must be considered.

Discretionary Access Control List (DACL)

A Discretionary Access Control List is a list of user accounts and group accounts that have authorization to use an object. An Access Control Entry (ACE) is a security mechanism that attaches a security identifier to permit or deny object access. The number of ACEs in a DACL is equal to the number of user and group accounts having permission to access the object. A System Access Control List (SACL) contains ACEs that are used for reviewing permissions. The number of ACEs in an SACL is equal to the number of user or group accounts. Access to a resource is granted if an access token has a SID. The SID matches the permission in the DACL associated with the access required. A deny ACE is an access control mechanism that rejects requests to access an object.

The access mask is a feature of the DACL that acknowledges the services of the reviewed account. Access to a resource is granted if an access token has a SID that matches the permission in the DACL. If any user wants to access a file, the system will grant permission only by comparing the access token of the executing program to the DACL attached to the file. If a security descriptor has no DACL (also known as a null DACL), this will give unconditional access to everyone; however, if a security descriptor exists, either explicit or inherited, with an empty DACL, it will deny access to everyone.

Objects and Permissions

Permissions are entries in DACLs. Data structures such as files, folders, directories, and shares are known as objects. Some of the fundamental operations that can be performed on an object are open, read, write, and delete.

Information about ownership and access control of an object is stored in that object's security descriptor. The components of a security descriptor are:

- *Owner*: The owner section of the security descriptor contains information about the owner of the object and the SID of the user account. The owner of the object can change the entries of the object's DACL to restrict the usage of the object.
- *Group*: This section has the SID of the object's group and is used only by the POSIX subsystems of Windows.

- *Discretionary Access Control List*: The DACL lists the permissions for object access. All user accounts and group accounts that have permission to access the object are listed here.
- *System Access Control List*: The SACL is used to monitor system objects.

User Rights

Activities that a user can carry out on many or all system objects are called user rights. User rights are required to perform actions that affect many objects together, such as shutting down the system or putting it to sleep.

Local Unique Identifiers (LUIDs) are associated with access tokens by the Local System Authority to grant user rights. The LUID consists of individual user rights and group user rights. Information about system security and user permissions is stored in the Security Manager Database, which is used for creating these LUIDs.

NTFS File System Permissions

New Technology File System (NTFS) is the basic file system of Windows operating systems. It offers a level of security by preventing illegal access to system resources. NTFS confirms the authenticity of the ACL associated with files for granting access to resources.

The CACLS (Change Access Control Lists) command-prompt tool handles access permissions. Using the CACLS command-prompt tool, objects can be edited to insert or remove specific permissions without affecting existing permissions. To manage NTFS file system permissions, an administrator can right-click on the file or folder from Windows Explorer, click **Properties**, and then click the **Security** tab.

Encryption File System (EFS)

EFS is a file system driver that can encrypt and decrypt files during transmission. It determines permissions for user access of any computer object alongside NTFS permissions. EFS uses public and private keys to encrypt files and folders. All users must do is select the *encrypted* attribute for the file. The files are decrypted when an NTFS file system driver requests them.

EFS has the following benefits:

- Disk drives cannot be accessed directly.
- EFS drivers run in kernel mode.
- EFS can be managed with little effort.
- EFS is transparent to users.
- Only required files or folders can be encrypted.
- No one can access the data without the private key.

One disadvantage of working with EFS is that only individual users on client systems can use it. Encrypted certifications for files are generated based on the identity of the users and can be used only by the account holders. EFS also faces problems during the decryption, creation, and deletion of files, because it requires extensive CPU usage and can be quite slow for each of those processes. Therefore, third-party encryption tools should also be used.

Windows Network Security

Windows provides many effective methods and tools for securing systems and networks. It uses the following services for security:

- *Active Directory*: Active Directory is a repository of all the information required for network security, including encryption keys and security certificates.
- *Kerberos*: Kerberos is a protocol to authenticate the clients and hosts in an open network.
- *Group policy*: Group policies are specifications for configurations of system tools.
- *Share security*: Shares are the information packets allowed to be shared between users.
- *IPSec*: IPSec uses cryptographic and filtering techniques to protect the network from attack.

These services work together to maintain Windows network security. The group policies of Active Directory specify the IPSec. A properly configured IPSec uses Kerberos for private-key exchanges. Share security depends on password hashes present in Active Directory, which are confirmed by Kerberos.

Security Modes of Operation

Modes of operation are usually categorized based on the information being processed and the clearance level of AIS. The four different modes of operations are:

1. Dedicated security mode
2. System high security mode
3. Compartmented security mode
4. Multilevel security mode

Dedicated Security Mode

In this mode, the system is dedicated to and is controlled by a particular type of process or classification of information, either permanently or for a particular period of time. In this mode, the AIS can handle a single classification level or category of information.

System High Security Mode

In this mode of operation, the system's hardware or software is guaranteed to provide need-to-know protection between users. The entire system includes all components that are electrically and physically connected. This mode should operate with security measures that match the classification and the sensitivity of the information being processed and stored.

In this mode, the users who access the AIS process will have the necessary security clearance or authorization for the information handled by that AIS.

Compartmented Security Mode

In compartmented security mode, the system is allowed to process two or more types of compartmented information.

Multilevel Security Mode

Multilevel security mode allows two or more classification levels of information to process simultaneously within the same system. This is useful when some users do not have the clearance or formal access approval for all information handled by the system.

Automated Information System (AIS)

An automated information system (AIS) is a complete system, including computer hardware, software, firmware, or any combination of the three. It is configured to perform specific information-handling operations:

- Automatic acquisition
- Storage
- Manipulation
- Management
- Movement
- Control
- Display
- Switching
- Interchange
- Transmission or reception of data

Windows Infrastructure Features

Active Directory

Active Directory is a collection of security information, such as certificates and crypto keys, distributed between domain controllers. It is, in effect, a complete list of every object in the Active Directory domain, and every attribute of those objects. This includes user accounts, system accounts, and administrative information of a network. An Active Directory's objects are associated with an ACL file, whose authenticity is confirmed before granting access to a resource.

Active Directory stores all directory information in an ISO X.500 protocol-based centralized database. This centralized information allows efficient management of system objects. The domain controller periodically updates all the information of Active Directory.

Active Directory provides information for the network, users, and administrators. It can also store and distribute application data over the network for the use of multiple applications. It enables network administrators to control any system on the network.

Active Directory includes domain controllers and domains, which enable the networks to adjust for differing requirements. Active Directory supports Lightweight Directory Access Protocol (LDAP) for easy access of directory information. Object names in Active Directory are compatible with Domain Name System (DNS), so IP-based names can be assigned.

Group Policy

Group policies are the set of configuration changes made for any specific purpose. They define the configuration settings for any group, such as security groups or members of any particular department.

The group policy deals with controlling changes in security setups and user management. It includes administrative privileges like enabling or disabling the permissions of users.

System configuration policies controlled by group policies include:

- Windows installer package distribution
- Registry settings
- Startup/shutdown scripts
- NTFS permissions
- Public-key policies
- IPSec policies
- System, network, and Windows components settings
- Services startup
- Registry permissions

User configuration policies controlled by group policies include:

- Windows Installer
- Logon/logoff scripts
- Internet Explorer settings
- System settings
- Network settings
- Remote Installation Service
- Start menu, taskbar, desktop, and Control Panel settings
- Windows components
- Security settings

The files and settings that are loaded at logon are called Group Policy Objects. These objects are stored in the SysVol share and consist of a computer policy and a user policy. These two parts must be configured separately. The computer policy is loaded during the startup of the computer, while the user policy varies from user to user and is loaded when a specific user logs on.

Computer policies manage operating system functionality, and similar policies can be applied to all the computers in the network. On the other hand, user policies vary depending on the accessibility rights given to the specific user. No matter what physical computer system the user is accessing, the user policy offers the same privileges. Group policies vary based on the security group or Active Directory container group to which the user belongs. The policy that affects the user is the one that is last applied on the system. The order in which group policies are applied is as follows:

- *Local machine*: This group policy is the first to be applied on the system and is downloaded from the Active Directory.

- *Site*: Computers can be located in any subnet of the company. The group policy varies based on the location of the computer on the network.

- *Domain*: This policy is applied to the entire network. For example, for the user to log on to the computer, a valid user account is required. This policy applies to the entire domain network.

- *Organizational unit*: All users have specific policies assigned to them.

A group policy can be applied as a whole, or a few features can be enabled to form a new policy.

Dynamic DNS Update

Windows Server 2003 provides the following features related to the dynamic DNS update protocol:

- Use of Active Directory locator service for domain controllers

- *Integration with Active Directory*: Integrating DNS zones into Active Directory provides increased fault tolerance and security. Every Active Directory–integrated zone is replicated among all domain controllers in the Active Directory domain. All DNS servers that are running on these domain controllers can act as primary servers for the zone and accept dynamic updates. Active Directory replicates on a per-property basis and propagates only relevant changes.

- *Aging and scavenging of records*: The DNS server service can scan and remove records that are no longer required. Enabling this feature can prevent outdated records from remaining in DNS.

- *Secure dynamic updates in Active Directory–integrated zones*: Active Directory–integrated zones can be configured for secure dynamic updates so that only authorized users can make changes to a zone or to a record.

- Administration from a command prompt

- Enhanced name resolution

- Enhanced caching and negative caching

- Interoperability with other DNS server implementations

- Integration with other network services

- Incremental zone transfer

Kerberos Authentication and Domain Security

Kerberos is a Windows and UNIX authentication protocol to check the authenticity of client and server computers in an open network. This authentication is done with the help of secure encryption keys. It uses shared secret keys stored in the Key Distribution Center (KDC) and acts as a trusted third party. The server and the client identify each other's authenticity based on these keys.

Authentication through Kerberos occurs through these steps:

1. The client and the server request the KDC to authenticate each other by sending the name of the other party.

2. The KDC checks the secret keys of the client and the server, and generates random session keys known as tickets.

3. Kerberos authenticates clients based on two tickets generated in encrypted form by the KDC. Valid clients can decrypt these keys and proceed to communicate with the server.

4. A client requests authentication of the server.

5. The KDC verifies its credentials from its central data repository.

6. Based on the time stamp and its details, an initial ticket is generated for the client. It comprises the session and is encrypted with its private key.

7. Based on the session key and accessibility credentials described in the administrative privileges, a secondary key is generated and encrypted using the server's private key.

8. The clients are granted access every time a request is made. The session is destroyed after each request. Every request results in a completely new connection.

The server initially validates the client's request by decrypting it with the server's shared key, and then with the client's private key from the KDC. A ticket expires after 10 hours by default, although this can be changed.

Kerberos services can be divided into two parts: the TGT service, which authenticates client and server using Active Directory, and the TGS, which generates session tickets for a valid TGT.

Trust Relationships Between Domains

A domain acts like a container in which the administrator can create logical groups of objects. The collection of domain user accounts is stored in Active Directory. Active Directory provides the tree structure for parent and child domains. Interdomain keys are created for Kerberos between parent and child domains if they are members of the same Active Directory. The relationship between these domains depends upon interdomain keys. Security principles are contained within these domains.

The domain that is trying to gain access is the client, and the domain the client is trying to access is the target domain. If the security principle in the parent domain wishes to access the security principle in the child domain, or vice versa, then the following process is followed:

1. The client approaches the local Key Distribution Center and sends a session ticket request.

2. The KDC finds the target in the local domain.

3. If the target is not present in the local domain, the KDC provides a session ticket to the client, which is encrypted by an interdomain key.

4. The client sends a request for a session ticket from the foreign KDC using the session ticket acquired from the local KDC.

5. Using the interdomain key, the foreign KDC decrypts the session ticket. The interdomain key provides the trust relationship between the domain controller and the client.

6. The foreign KDC gives the session key to the client for the foreign target server.

If the security principle in one domain wishes to access the security principle in another distant domain, which may be two hops away or more in the Active Directory domain hierarchy, then the following process is followed:

1. A client sends a request for a session ticket for the target server to its KDC.

2. The KDC provides the referral ticket of the next adjacent domain.

3. A client sends a request for a session key using this referral ticket.

4. The KDC again provides the referral ticket of the next adjacent domain.

5. This process continues until the target domain is not found.

6. The client accesses the session key for authentication of the target security principle.

IP Security (IPSec)

IPSec policy rules are used for secure communication among computers. Windows is configured using IPSec. Default IP security rules help to both configure client systems for allowing encryption and configure server systems for requesting encryption.

The requesting encryption server can communicate only with authenticated clients. These clients must possess a legal Security Association (SA) that goes hand in hand with Internet Key Exchange (IKE).

A Windows host can encrypt the communication stream between itself and other hosts. It cannot encrypt communications between two private networks like a bastion host. Windows allows the communication only in transfer mode and not in ESP tunnel mode. In transfer mode, it supports Authenticated Headers (AH) and Encapsulating Security Payload (ESP). Internet Key Exchange (IKE) provides encryption keys and protocols to Windows hosts.

Windows uses one of the following private keys for IKE authentication:

- *Kerberos tickets*: These are used by hosts running Windows or higher. Kerberos domains provide session tickets capable of perfect IPSec authentication for the same domain hosts.

- *Certificates*: These are useful for extranets. They can be used when:

  - Domains are not using trusted communication

- Communicating with non-Windows hosts
- Using public key infrastructure (PKI)
- *Manual secret keys*: These are useful for the encryption of communications among hosts not present in a PKI environment or domain. In a PKI environment, communication with non-Windows hosts is possible.

Problems with IPSec

IPSec is becoming the solution for all security problems. It is helpful for various security issues, but it has some problems, including:

- It is incompatible with other important security mechanisms such as NAT and proxy servers.
- It removes the filtering ability of firewalls based on packet types, because it does not allow firewalls to see TCP and UDP packets.
- It consumes a good deal of processing time and power.

Due to this, IPSec is not becoming the host-to-host security service for the transport mode of Windows, but it is becoming the network-to-network encryption service for tunnel mode of VPN devices. It is most useful in secure administrator-to-public host connections and in secure communication for public networks.

Windows 2003 Infrastructure, Authentication, and Auditing

Authentication

IIS 6.0 introduced a new authentication mechanism known as Advanced Digest Authentication. When this authentication is used, the credentials of the users are stored in Active Directory on the domain controller as an MD5 message.

Because Advance Digest Authentication relies on HTTP 1.1, it is not supported by all browsers. Earlier browsers must have the actual username and password, so the information must be stored in a reversible encryption format for those browsers to function. MD5 by its nature is not reversible.

To enable Advanced Digest Authentication on an IIS server, an administrator can configure the properties of the Web site folder, specific Web site, and directories using the following steps:

1. Right-click the object, and click the **Security** tab.
2. Click the **Edit** button in the **Authentication and Access Control** section.
3. In the **Authentication Methods** dialog box, check the **Digest authentication for Windows domain servers** check box in the **Authenticated access** section, as shown in Figure 3-3.
4. A dialog box will state that Digest Authentication works with Active Directory Domain Accounts. Click the **Yes** button.
5. In the **Realm** dialog box, type a **Realm Name** and click the **OK** button.

Security Configuration Tools

The Security Configuration Wizard (SCW) was introduced in Windows Server 2003 to help administrators create, test, deploy, and manage policies. The SCW cannot be used to configure domain-level policies because it is not integrated with Active Directory. With the help of an SCW prototype, policies can be easily created. These prototype policies are made for multiple server roles. The SCW can automatically manage registry settings, Windows firewall exceptions, and service settings, as well as deploy rollback policies. The command-line tool scwcmd allows the SCW and the group policy to be used together for the deployment of policies to groups of computers or to convert the policies to Group Policy Objects (GPOs).

Security Configuration Editor

Security Configuration Editor tools are used to define security policy templates applied to individual computers or to groups of computers through the Active Directory group policy.

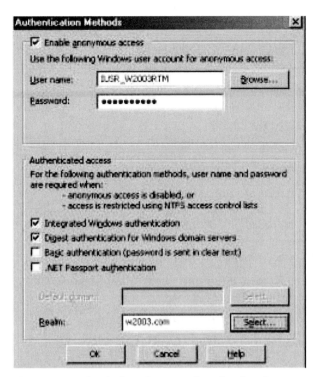

Figure 3-3 Check the **Digest authentication for Windows domain servers** check box.

Active Directory Users and Computers

The Active Directory Users console and the computer snap-in provide a graphical interface for the creation and management of organizational units within the domain. GPOs and OUs (organizational units) that control policy order and inheritance can be linked.

Group Policy Management Console

The Group Policy Management Console (GPMC) controls the group policy for a large environment. The GPMC provides the following:

- A user interface that focuses on group policy use and management
- The ability to quickly back up, restore, import, export, copy, and paste GPOs
- Simplified management of group policy–related security
- Report capabilities for GPO and Resultant Set of Policy (RSoP) data
- Scriptable GPO operations

Resource Security

In system management, server security is maintained by creating security rights that specify the user and user group permissions for various objects such as collections, packages, advertisements, and status objects. Security rights can also be created for the entire collection or for specific instances. A collection can be created that contains the target resource, and then permission is granted to it so that a user can only access that specific collection. Excluding other SMSs, object permissions can also be granted for the resources in a collection, including deleting resources, modifying resources, reading resources, using remote tools, and viewing collected files. Permission cannot be granted for a single resource in a collection; if permission is granted to a user for a resource in a collection, then that permission extends for the same resource contained in another collection.

Auditing and Logging

Windows Server 2003 auditing tracks user and system activities. When auditing is used, events such as valid and invalid logon attempts and events that are related to the opening, creating, and deleting of files or objects are written to a security log. The audit entry in the security log contains the following information:

- The action performed
- The user who performed the action
- The success or failure of the event
- The time the event occurred

When Active Directory events are audited, an event is written by Windows Server 2003 to the security log on the domain controller. When a user wants to log on to the domain using a domain user account and the logon attempt fails, this event is recorded on the domain controller. It is not recorded on the specific computer where the unsuccessful logon attempt is made. To view the event, Event Viewer is used.

To configure an audit policy setting for a domain controller, an administrator can follow these steps:

1. Click the **Start** button, then **Programs**, then **Administrative Tools**, and click **Active Directory Users and Computers**.
2. On the **View** menu, click **Advanced Features**.
3. Right-click **Domain Controllers** and then click **Properties**.
4. Click the **Group Policy** tab, click **Default Domain Controller Policy**, and then click **Edit**.
5. Click **Computer Configuration**, double-click **Windows Settings**, double-click **Security Settings**, double-click **Local Policies**, and then double-click **Audit Policy**.
6. In the right pane, right-click **Audit Directory Services Access**, and then click **Properties**.
7. Click **Define These Policy Settings**, and then check one or both of the following check boxes:
   - Success: Check this check box to audit successful attempts for the event category.
   - Failure: Check this check box to audit failed attempts for the event category.
8. Right-click any other event category that you want to audit, and then click **Properties**.
9. Click the **OK** button.
10. The changes made to the computer's audit policy settings take effect only when the policy setting is propagated or applied to the computer. Complete either of the following steps to initiate policy propagation:
    - Type **gpupdate /target: computer** at the command prompt and then press Enter.
    - Wait for automatic policy propagation that occurs at regular intervals. By default, the policy propagation occurs every 5 minutes.
11. Open the Security log to view logged events.

Windows 2003 EFS

Windows Server 2003 provides significant advancements in data recovery and protection and private key recovery. The EFS in the Windows Server 2003 supports the use of Data Recovery Agents (DRA) to decrypt files that are encrypted by other users.

EFS File Sharing

The use of EFS file sharing in Windows 2003 allows additional users to view encrypted files. When a file is encrypted, sharing is enabled through a new button in the user interface. After choosing the advanced properties of the encrypted file, a new user can be added by clicking the **Detail** button.

To encrypt a file for multiple users, an administrator can follow these steps:

1. Open Windows Explorer and select the file to be encrypted.
2. Right-click the chosen file and click **Properties**.
3. Select the **Advanced** button to enable EFS.

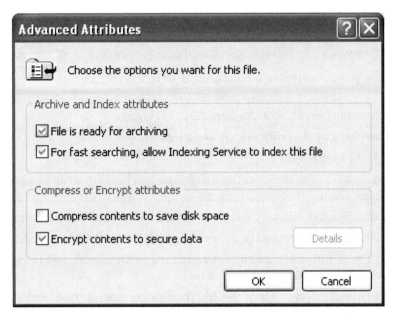

Figure 3-4   Check the **Encrypt contents to secure data** check box.

4. Encrypt the file by checking the **Encrypt contents to secure data** check box shown in Figure 3-4. Click the **OK** button. A file cannot be both compressed and encrypted at the same time. If this is the first time this file or folder has been encrypted, a dialog box will appear asking if only the file should be encrypted, or the whole folder.

5. Select the appropriate choice and click the **OK** button. This will return to the original dialog box. The file is not encrypted until the **OK** button is clicked. Also, additional users may not be added until the file has been encrypted by the first user.

6. Open the file properties again with the **Advanced Properties** button and then click the **Details** button to add additional users. Once the **Details** dialog box is open, the **Add user** option will be displayed.

Windows 2003 Network Security

The network has different local policies that affect both the clients' and the servers' network security. The following security options are listed under the network security configuration:

- Do not store the LAN manager hash value on the next password change.
- Force a logoff when the logon hours expire.
- LAN manager-authentication level
- LDAP client-signing requirement
- Minimum session security for NTLM SSP-based client
- Minimum session security NTLM SSP-based server

These policies are located under Computer Settings Windows Settings Security Settings Local Policies Security Options in the Microsoft Management Console (MMC) Group Policy Object Editor snap-in. The options for these security settings are:

- Require message integrity
- Require message confidentiality
- Require NTLM version 2 session security
- Require 128-bit encryption

By default, there are no requirements for these settings.

Windows Certification Authorities

To import a CA certificate from Microsoft Certificate Services, an administrator can follow these steps:

1. On the computer requiring a CA certificate, open Internet Explorer.

2. In Internet Explorer, connect to *http://<servername>/certsrv*, where *<servername>* is the name of the server where the Certification Authority (CA) is located.

3. Click **Download a CA certificate, certificate chain, or CRL**.

4. Do one of the following:

   - To trust all the certificates issued by this certification authority (CA), click **Install this CA certificate chain**.

   - If the certification authority has been renewed, choose a version of the CA certificate to download.

   - Select the encoding method you want for the CRL: DER (Distinguished Encoding Rules) or Base64.

   - Under **CA Certificate**, click the CA certificate to download, and then click **Download CA certificate** or click **Download CA certificate chain**.

   - In **File Download**, click **Open this file from its current location**, and then click **OK**.

   - When the **Certificate** dialog box appears, click **Install this certificate**.

   - In the **Certificate Import** wizard, click **Automatically selects the certificate store based on the type of certificate**. This places the CA certificate in the **Trusted Root Store**.

5. When finished using the Certificate Services Web pages, close Internet Explorer.

To install the certificate of the enterprise root CA as a trusted root CA certificate, an administrator can follow these steps:

1. Open **Active Directory Users and Computers**.

2. In the console tree, double-click **Active Directory Users and Computers**, right-click the domain name in which the CA lives, and then click **Properties**.

3. On the **Group Policy** tab, click **Default Domain Policy**, and then click **Edit**.

4. In the console tree, right-click **Trusted Root Certification Authorities**, point to **All Tasks**, and then click **Import**. CA is located in Computer Configuration/Windows Settings/Security Settings/Public Key Policies/Trusted Root Certification Authorities. The Certificate Manager Import wizard should now appear.

5. Click **Next** and follow the instructions in the wizard to import the .crt file of the CA (located in the systemroot System 32 CertSrv CertEnroll folder) into the Trusted Root Certification Authorities store.

6. Type the following at the command prompt:

```
gpupdate /target:{computer | user} /force
```

Desktop Management

Desktop management consists of overseeing laptops, computing devices, and desktop computers. As a part of systems management, it controls all the components of an organization's information system.

The major tasks of desktop management include:

- Installing and maintaining hardware and software
- Spam filtering
- Managing user permissions

Concept of Least Privilege

The concept of least privilege states that each subject in a system, be it a user or process, should be granted the most restrictive set of privileges (or lowest clearance) required for the performance of authorized tasks. This will reduce the damage or failure that may result from accident, error, or unauthorized use.

Internal Labeling

During the creation of records, accurate labeling is required in order to retrieve electronically stored records. External tape labels must include:

- Data
- File title(s)
- Date of creation and coverage
- Recording density (number of bits or characters recorded per inch (bpi) or (cpi))
- Type of internal labels, if applicable
- Volume series number
- Number of tracks and track bit assignments
- Character code/software dependency
- Record length
- Block size (e.g., fixed, variable, or mixed)
- Disposition instructions
- Reel sequence if the file is part of a multireel set
- Security determination

Disk labels should include:

- File or subject name and/or number
- Date, if appropriate
- Software and equipment dependency
- Disposition instructions

Files that cannot be identified due to poor external or internal labeling are not useful, so the filenames should be as recognizable as possible.

Securing Linux

User Administration

Most Linux systems are configured with a graphical user interface. The graphical login screen has login options and fields to enter a username and password. Once logged in, the user can choose to use a graphical user interface or a command line.

The Linux system supports a multiuser environment, but the system cannot be accessed directly. The interface is a shell through which interaction is possible. The Linux system is capable of maintaining several shells at one time that can control several users simultaneously. Linux is a form of UNIX, which was first used in computers such as mainframes and is made to accommodate several hundred users. User accounts are created by the system administrator. A tool such as system-config-user is used for the configuration of user accounts. There are some conventions for creating and maintaining user accounts, including:

- Passwords should be easy to remember
- Password aging and shadow files should be used
- All user accounts must have passwords
- File permissions should be restricted
- Xlock and xscreensaver should be used
- PAM (Pluggable Authentication Module) should be used

File System Security

The Linux file system is organized as a tree structure, storing all files with their location addresses in a hierarchical format. The directory tree of Linux is composed of many file systems stored on different storage devices.

The layout and organization of the system directories is described by the Filesystem Hierarchy Standard (FHS). The Linux system has to follow this standard while setting up the system directories. Configuration files should be stored in the /etc directory, while device files should be in the /dev directory. The root directory for the file system is denoted with a slash.

Newer versions of Linux have a journaling feature, which helps users recover from crashes.

Data Security and Network Security

Data security in Linux is achieved using several mechanisms, including encryption, integrity checks, and digital signatures. GNU Privacy Guard encryption helps protect outbound mail and files, and digital signatures help authenticate messages.

Data are encrypted using a systematic approach to send the data over the network. The sender encrypts the data with a key so the receiver can later decrypt the data. This also ensures that the data are not modified during transmission. It is important to check that the data are transmitted from the actual sender, because the encryption and integrity check protect the data but do not authenticate the sender.

Public-Key Encryption

Encryption is usually done using one key both to encrypt and decrypt. If any other person knows the key, the data can be decrypted easily. Public-key encryption uses two keys for the encryption and decryption of data: one is the private key and the other is the public key. The private key is kept on both ends and is used to decrypt the data, while the encryption is done with the public key.

Digital Signatures

A digital signature checks the authenticity and integrity of a message. The digital signature is combined with the encrypted message to provide greater security.

Integrity Check

The message generates a checksum value from the content of the message. This value is generated by the encryption hash algorithm. The checksum is a unique value that represents the size and the content of the message.

Linux Update Agent

Linux Update Agent keeps the operating system up to date. It communicates over the Internet to a central server and download applicable software patches. It also performs automatic installation of downloaded patches. Update Agents are required to maintain security by updating the different security software tools.

To configure the application, an administrator selects **Configure** in the main dialog box. The **Configuration** dialog box presents a three-tabbed window for the following information to be entered:

- *User*: Enter the desired username and password, along with an e-mail address where update notifications can be sent.

- *Retrieval*: Specify the name of the server and installation instructions, such as the version of Linux to update and where to install the downloaded packages.

- *Exceptions*: This specifies the files and/or packages that need to be excluded from the update search, such as kernel-related files.

Configuring Linux Services

Removal of unnecessary programs running on the Linux computer is important to minimize vulnerabilities. Linux runs many system programs on bootup. These programs are known as services or daemons. Linux supports many functions and background processes such as sendmail, chargen, wine, and snmpd. These daemons run in different modes, defined by the administrator. Some services must be made available to all users in common run levels, and others should run in restricted run levels for limited access by system administrators. The important run levels are numbered as follows:

- *0 (Halt)*: Shuts down the system

- *1 (Single-user mode)*: User can access the system only with root-level rights; designed for maintenance and software installation

- *3 (Multiuser mode—text)*: Permits multiple users to log on with the command-line interface, enabling remote file sharing
- *5 (Multiuser mode—graphical)*: Starts in X Window mode, allowing multiple users to log on
- *6 (Reboot)*: Reboots the system

Administrators should configure the operating system to start only the required services at bootup. Deleting these services will stop them from running. The chkconfig command is used to add and delete running services. The serviceconf and ntsysv commands are used to configure the services.

User Management

Various tools are used to manage user accounts and their passwords. In Linux, users must have user accounts with unique identities so that the actions of each user can be identified. Tools used to manage user accounts in Linux include:

- *useradd*: This establishes a user account using command-line options.
- *usermod*: This modifies existing user accounts.
- *userdel*: This deletes existing user accounts.
- *passwd*: This changes the password of an existing user account.

Password Security

Passwords are the fields where Linux verifies that users logging into the system are who they claim to be. Linux uses MD5 (Message Digest Algorithm 5) and shadow passwords.

If MD5 is not selected during installation, the older Data Encryption Standard (DES) format is used. This format restricts the passwords to eight alphanumeric characters and provides 56-bit encryption.

If a shadow password is not selected, all user passwords are stored in a one-way hash in the world-readable file /etc/passwd. This leaves the system open to offline password cracking attacks.

Creating Strong Passwords

While creating passwords, do not:

- Use only words or numbers
- Use recognizable words
- Use words in foreign languages
- Use hacker terminology
- Use personal information
- Invert recognizable words
- Write down the password
- Use the same password for all machines

Do:

- Make the password at least eight characters long
- Mix uppercase and lowercase letters
- Mix letters and numbers
- Include nonalphanumeric characters
- Pick a memorable password

Shadow Password

It is necessary to use a shadow password when working in a multiuser environment. Shadow passwords are provided by the shadow-utils package. By default, shadow passwords are enabled.

Advantages of shadow passwords include:

- Encrypted passwords are moved from world-readable /etc/passwd file to /etc/shadow, which can only be accessed by the root user.
- They store information about password aging.
- They use the /etc/login.defs file to enforce security policies.

Password-aging information is stored in the /etc/shadow file. Commands that create or modify the password-aging information will not work. There are some commands that will not work without enabling shadow passwords first, including:

- change
- gpasswd
- /usr/sbin/usermod -e or -f options
- /usr/sbin/useradd -e or -f options

etc/passwd

The file /etc/passwd contains user accounts, attributes, and associated passwords. Within the file, each user account is listed on a separate line with different fields and symbols. A colon separates each user attribute. The drawback of this file is that all users have read permissions to the file. The different fields are as follows:

- *Username*: This is the name of the user.
- *Password*: Passwords are passed through the encryption algorithm. The encrypted password is stored in this file.
- *User ID (UID)*: This unique identification number determines the access rights of the user account.
- *Group ID (GID)*: This determines whether the members of a group have access rights to files or applications.
- *GECOS*: This holds user information and the comments associated with users.
- *Home directory*: This is the location of the user's home directory, where the user can store personal information.
- *Shell*: This is the default command-line interface that allows the user to interact with the operating system.

etc/shadow

The /etc/shadow/ file is a password file hidden inside the operating system. Access to this file is restricted to users with administrative access. The following are the fields in /etc/shadow:

- *Username*: This is the name specified to enter the Linux operating system.
- *Password*: Passwords are passed through the encryption algorithm. The encrypted password is stored in this file.
- *Date password last changed*: This is the number of days since the password was last changed.
- *Minimum number of days password before a password change*: This is the minimum number of days required between password changes.
- *Maximum number of days before password change is required*: The password must be changed before this number of days is up.
- *Number of days of warning before password change*: When this number of days passes, the user will be told that the password must be changed.
- *Number of days before account is disabled*: This is the number of days that the user can go without changing the password after it has expired. If this number passes, the account is disabled, and an administrator must recreate the account.
- *Reserve field*: This field is currently empty.

etc/gshadow

The /etc/gshadow file preserves the group information and can be accessed only by administrators. It has the following fields:

- *Group name*: This is the name of the group.
- *Encrypted password*: This is the encrypted version of the group password. To become a member of the group, a user must have access to the password.
- *Group administrators*: This is a comma-separated list of the users who can add or delete group members.
- *Member list*: This is a comma-separated list of the users who belong to the group.

etc/group

Groups are hosted in the /etc/group file. Numerous groups are installed by default on a Linux system. The fields in this file are:

- *Group name*: This is the name of the group.
- *Group password*: This is the encrypted version of the group password. A user who wants to become a member of this group must have access to the password.
- *GID*: This is used to recognize the group and analyze if its members have access to the requested assets.
- *Member list*: This is a comma-separated list of the users who belong to the group.

File System and Navigation

The files in Linux are arranged in a hierarchical structure. They are organized in a tree pattern, as shown in Figure 3-5. The topmost directory in the file system is the root directory. All the files, directories, and subdirectories are under the root directory.

The command-line interface does not show graphical pictures of the file system structure. There are files and subdirectories within a directory. The directory that the prompt displays is the current (working) directory. To see the present working directory, a user can use the pwd command. The ls command lists the files in the working directory. Table 3-2 shows some of the options of the ls command.

Figure 3-6 shows sample output of **ls -l**.

To change the working directory, the cd command is used followed by the pathname of the desired working directory. There are two ways to give the pathname: the absolute pathname and the relative pathname. The absolute pathname starts from the root directory and gives information about the end path of the file or the

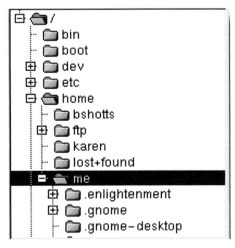

Figure 3-5 The Linux file system is organized in a tree pattern.

Command	Result
ls	Lists the files in the working directory
ls /bin	Lists the files in the /bin directory
ls -l	Lists the files in the working directory in long format
ls -l /etc /bin	Lists the files in the /bin directory and the /etc directory in long format
ls -la ..	Lists all files, even those normally hidden, in the parent of the working directory in long format

Table 3-2   These are some of the ls command's options

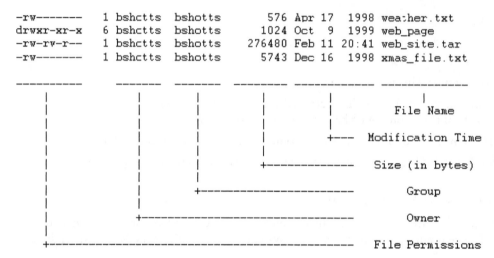

Figure 3-6   This is output of **ls -l.**

directory. A relative pathname specifies the path relative to the current directory. A single dot (.) used after cd refers to the current directory, and two dots (..) refers to the parent directory.

The following is an example of cd using absolute pathnames:

```
tn]$ cd /usr/X11R6

[me@linuxbox X11R6]$ pwd

/usr/X11R6
```

The following is an example of cd using relative pathnames:

```
[me@linuxbox bin]$ cd ..

[me@linuxbox X11R6]$ pwd

/usr/X11R6
```

Default Directories

To efficiently manage Linux security, system administrators and security professionals need to know these existing default directories:

- */(root file system)*: Functions as an origin from which all other directories can be accessed
- */bin*: Contains commands or binary files that should be accessible to all users
- */boot*: Contains files essential to the boot process
- */dev*: Contains device files that must be employed to access a range of system devices
- */etc*: Contains essential configuration files

- */home*: Contains user home directories
- */lib*: Contains application library files and kernel modules
- */mnt*: Other file systems such as floppy and CD-ROM drives can be mounted and accessed from this directory
- */opt*: Contains supplementary third-party applications and nonobligatory software
- */root*: Home directory for the root account
- */sbin*: Contains system commands and other utilities accessible to the system administrator
- */tmp*: Contains temporary files that are not required to be stored for future use on the system
- */usr*: Contains a huge hierarchy of files and directories that are accessible to system users
- */var*: Contains a huge hierarchy of files and directories that store a range of applications and system data such as printer spool files and log files

Interface Configuration Files

Interface configuration files control the software interfaces for individual network devices. As the system boots, it uses these files to determine what interfaces to select and how to configure them. These files are usually named *ifcfg-<name>*, where *<name>* refers to the name of the device that the configuration file controls.

Ethernet Interfaces

One of the most common interface files is ifcfg-eth0, which controls the first Ethernet network interface card (NIC) in the system. In a system with multiple NICs, there are multiple ifcfg-eth *<X>* files (where *<X>* is a unique number corresponding to a specific interface). As each device has its own configuration file, an administrator can control how each interface functions.

The following is a sample ifcfg-eth0 file for a system using a fixed IP address:

```
DEVICE=eth0

BOOTPROTO=none

ONBOOT=yes

NETWORK=10.0.1.0

NETMASK=255.255.255.0

IPADDR=10.0.1.27

USERCTL=no
```

The values required in an interface configuration file can change based on other values. For example, the ifcfg-eth0 file for an interface using DHCP looks quite a bit different, because IP information is provided by the DHCP server:

```
DEVICE=eth0

BOOTPROTO=dhcp

ONBOOT=yes
```

The Network Administration Tool can be used to make changes to the various network interface configuration files. It is also possible to edit the configuration files for a given network interface by hand. The following is a listing of the configurable parameters in an Ethernet interface configuration file:

- BOOTPROTO=<protocol>, where <protocol> is one of the following:
  - none: No boot-time protocol should be used
  - bootp: The BOOTP protocol should be used
  - dhcp: The DHCP protocol should be used
- BROADCAST=<address>, where <address> is the broadcast address; this parameter is deprecated

- DEVICE=<name>, where <name> is the name of the physical device (except for dynamically allocated PPP devices, where it is the logical name)
- DNS{1,2}=<address>, where <address> is a name server address to be placed in /etc/resolv.conf if the PEERDNS directive is set to yes
- IPADDR=<address>, where <address> is the IP address
- NETMASK=<mask>, where <mask> is the netmask value
- NETWORK=<address>, where <address> is the network address; this parameter is deprecated
- ONBOOT=<answer>, where <answer> is one of the following:
    - yes: This device should be activated at boot time
    - no: This device should not be activated at boot time
- PEERDNS=<answer>, where <answer> is one of the following:
    - yes: Modify /etc/resolv.conf if the DNS directive is set; if using DCHP, yes is the default
    - no: Do not modify /etc/resolv.conf
- SRCADDR=<address>, where <address> is the specified source IP address for outgoing packets
- USERCTL=<answer>, where <answer> is one of the following:
    - yes: Nonroot users are allowed to control this device
    - no: Nonroot users are not allowed to control this device

Other Interfaces

Other common interface configuration files that use these options include the following:

- *ifcfg-lo*: A local loopback interface is often used in testing, as well as in a variety of applications that require an IP address pointing back to the same system. Any data sent to the loopback device is immediately returned to the host's network layer.
- *ifcfg-irlan0*: An infrared interface allows information between devices, such as a laptop and a printer, to flow over an infrared link. This works similar to an Ethernet device except that it commonly occurs over a peer-to-peer connection.
- *ifcfg-plip0*: A Parallel Line Interface Protocol (PLIP) connection works much the same way, except that it utilizes a parallel port.
- *ifcfg-tr0*: Token Ring topologies are not as common on LANs as they once were, having been replaced by Ethernet.

Alias and Clone Files

Two lesser-used types of interface configuration files found in the /etc/sysconfig/network-scripts directory are alias and clone files.

Alias interface configuration files are named in the format of *ifcfg-<if-name>:<alias-value>*, and they allow an alias to point to an interface. For example, an ifcfg-eth0:0 file could be configured to specify *DEVICE=eth0:0* and a static IP address of 10.0.0.2, serving as an alias of an Ethernet interface already configured to receive its IP information via DHCP in ifcfg-eth0. At that point, the eth0 device is bound to a dynamic IP address, but it can always be referred to on that system via the fixed 10.0.0.2 IP address.

A clone interface configuration file should follow this naming convention: *ifcfg-<if-name>-<clonename>*. While an alias file is another way to refer to an existing interface configuration file, a clone file is used to specify additional options when specifying an interface. For example, if there is a standard DHCP Ethernet interface called eth0, it may look similar to the following:

```
DEVICE=eth0

ONBOOT=yes

BOOTPROTO=dhcp
```

Because USERCTL is set to no if it is not specified, users cannot bring this interface up and down. To give them this ability, an administrator can create a clone by copying ifcfg-eth0 to ifcfg-eth0-user and adding the following line:

```
USERCTL=yes
```

When a user brings up the eth0 interface with the **ifup eth0-user** command, the configuration options from ifcfg-eth0 and ifcfg-eth0-user are combined. While this is a very basic example, this method can be used with a variety of options and interfaces.

Linux Certificate Authorities

The digital certificates used today are obtained from commercial CAs, which implement a number of standard practices and processes. The functions of certificate authorities are the same whether they are on an intranet or the Internet. The certificate authority performs some basic functions during the certificate's life cycle such as:

- Processing certificate requests to verify the identity of the requester and then issue a certificate that is prepared according to the policy for that CA
- Managing the certificate audit trail from the enrollment of the certificate to its expiration or revocation
- Renewing certificates before they expire
- Revoking certificates as necessary
- Maintaining and publishing certificate revocation lists (CRLs)

OpenLDAP

Lightweight Directory Access Protocol (LDAP) helps get data for individuals, system users, network devices, and applications that require authentication or information. OpenLDAP is an open-source implementation of LDAP for Linux.

Using CATool

Certificate authorities provide a self-signed certificate called the root certificate. Mostly, identity certificates are used, which provide information about systems, hosts, etc.

CATool is a private certificate authority tool. The basic process is to provide the user with authentication, managing the workflow of the request and signing process. The whole process is automated by a Web-based interface.

CATool is used by many categories of users, including:

- Administrators
- Signers
- Users

Pluggable Authentication Module

Pluggable Authentication Module (PAM) is used to control the function of various applications. It is a series of library modules that depend on configuration files for authentication of system users. It consists of many modules that are in /lib/security and the configuration files listed in the /etc/pam.d directory. Linux has features that enable administrators to manage authentication policies. Applications must be written to make use of PAM.

The locations of PAM configuration files and library modules are as follows:

- PAM applications are configured in the directory /etc/pam.d or in the file /etc/pam.conf.
- Library modules are stored in the directory /lib/security.
- Configuration files are located in the directory /etc/security.

Linux-PAM (Pluggable Authentication Modules for Linux) is a collection of shared libraries that enable the local system administrator to decide how applications will authenticate users. The function of the Linux-PAM project is to break up the development of privilege-granting software by the development of secure and appropriate authentication schemes. This is accomplished by providing a library of functions that an application uses to request user authentication. This PAM library is configured locally with a system file, /etc/pam.conf (or a series of configuration files located in /etc/pam.d/), to authenticate a user request via the locally available authentication modules. The modules are located in the directory /lib/security and take the form of dynamically loadable object files.

Without recompiling a PAM-aware application, it is possible to switch between the authentication mechanisms it uses. It can be used to upgrade the local authentication system without disturbing the applications.

PAM Configuration Files

The configuration files of PAM are stored in the /etc/pam.d directory. There may be a few files in this directory. There are some files that authenticate the user for each of the programs installed on the system. The following is a sample PAM configuration file for login:

```
/etc/pam.d/$ cat login

# PAM configuration for login

auth requisite pam_securetty.so

auth required pam_nologin.so

auth required pam_env.so

auth required pam_unix.so nullok

account required pam_unix.so

session required pam_unix.so

session optional pam_lastlog.so

password required pam_unix.so nullok obscure min=4 max=8
```

PAM Framework

PAM helps in plugging in new authentication technologies without requiring changes to applications. The system administrator can use any possible combination of services with PAM.

The PAM framework consists of the libraries, pluggable modules, and configuration files. The PAM application programming interface is implemented by the PAM library. This API serves to manage the PAM transaction and invokes the PAM Service Programming interface. The system administrator configures a system to use PAM through modification of the attribute auth_type. The command **auth_type=PAM_auth** configures a PAM-enabled command to invoke the PAM API directly for authentication. The commands that are categorized and have been modified for the recognition of the auth_type attribute are as follows:

- login
- passwd
- su
- ftp
- telnet
- rlogin
- rexec
- rsh
- snappd
- imapd
- dtaction
- dtlogin
- dtsession

Module	Configuration File	Description
pam_cracklib.so	/etc/pam.d/system-auth	Checks for password weakness, palindromes, recently used passwords, rotation, and other detectable features
pam_unix.so	/etc/pam.d/system-auth	Checks for authenticity of users on the basis of username, passwords, and its databases; establishes Syslog login sessions
pam_deny.so	/etc/pam.d/system-auth	Blocks the user's access to particular applications
pam_env.so	/etc/pam.d/system-auth	Modifies the environment variables
pam_nologin.so	/etc/pam.d/login	Checks for /etc/no login file to disallow nonroot logins
	/etc/pam.d/ppp	
	/etc/pam.d/xdm	
pam_ftp.so	/etc/pam.d/ftp	Controls authentication to wu_ftp application, if installed
pam_securetty.so	/etc/pam.d/login	Ensures that only users with root privileges can be logged on at the local console and others are disabled
pam_wheel.so	/etc/pam.d/su	Enables only wheel group members to access the su command
pam_limits.so	/etc/pam.d/system-auth	Controls allocating resources for each user, maximum file size, number of processes, and address space

Table 3-3 **PAM contains these modules**

PAM Modules

Table 3-3 shows the modules in PAM, along with their configuration files.

Network Information Service (NIS)

Network Information Service is a program developed by Sun Microsystems to permit PCs to share files consisting of passwords and user IDs to centrally administer user accounts. Linux supports this distributed user and password administration infrastructure. Network Information Service was revealed to be compromised due to the lack of host authentication mechanisms and transmitting information in plain text. Therefore, organizations must plan an NIS-facilitated UNIX infrastructure to guarantee that the confidential information is not compromised.

NIS, previously called Yellow Pages (YP), is a distributed database system that permits systems to share password files, group files, host tables, etc. over the network. NIS makes things easier in the administration of a network because the entire account and configuration information is restructured and accumulated on a single computer, the NIS master server. NIS can be incorporated with SunOS, the majority of SVR4 UNIX systems, and many other versions of UNIX.

Shared NIS database files are called maps, and hosts that fit into the same NIS domain share an identical set of maps. NIS slave servers, which gain the latest copies of the maps from the NIS master server, are used to present information when the NIS master server is not functioning properly.

NIS must be carefully configured to avoid serious security problems. NIS naming services were initially designed to tackle the administration requirements of client-server networks. These networks had definite characteristics, including:

- The capacity never went beyond 100 multivendor end-user desktops and a few servers for general usage.

- They extended to a maximum of only a few physically remote sites.

- They had secured and advanced users, so security was not a problem.

The file hosts.equiv can be restricted with NIS. Systems that are configured with NIS software from Sun Microsystems sometimes still have the default hosts.equiv file with a + as its single entry. This is a risk because the default hosts.equiv file considers all hosts to be secure.

NIS functions by having either of the lines +::0:0: or +: in the password or group file. When a program accesses the password or group file and comes across a line with a + as the first character, it interprets the plus sign as meaning that the program must ask the NIS server for the remainder of the file. Making use of the + ::0:0: format is a risk to the systems. If the leading + is deleted, an intruder can enter into the system with a null login name and gain priority access to the system.

The ypset command can be used to inform a process called ypbind where NIS requests need to be sent to a definite host. This feature was developed to permit debugging and to allow hosts that are not a part of the network with an NIS server to employ NIS. The ypset command creates a security problem, as it can be employed to direct requests to a fake NIS server.

NIS has map-building procedures to assist in leaving the maps world-writeable. Any skilled user can acquire copies of the databases exported by a NIS server. This can result in an accidental exposure of the distributed password file and other data present in the NIS database.

Group Management Utilities

Group management utilities manage the user groups of the system along with individual users. UNIX and Linux have some associated text-related utilities. The following utilities are used to administer groups and group membership:

- *groupadd*: This utility enables administrators to generate a new group.
- *groupdel*: This utility enables administrators to delete groups.
- *groupmod*: This utility helps administrators alter the properties of a group. For instance, the administrator can configure group passwords and add or delete group members.
- *usermod*: This facilitates changing group memberships for a specific user by using the -g command-line option and allows administrators to alter user account properties.

Permission Management Tools

Permission management tools are a range of tools that assist administrators in managing file and directory permissions on a system. For instance, major versions of UNIX come with the chmod command, which administrators can use to alter the permissions on files and directories. Its syntax is:

```
chmod <rights> <file>
```

The *file* argument represents the file or directory whose permissions will be modified. The *rights* argument represents the new permissions. There are different ways to represent permissions for the owner, group, and other users, and the number scheme is the simplest method. Permissions can be set using three numbers such as:

```
chmod 148 sample.txt
```

The first number represents the rights that should be allocated to the owner of the file. The second number represents the rights that should be allocated to the possessing group. The final number represents the rights granted to all other users. These numbers come from the following list:

- 7: Full rights (read, write and execute)
- 6: Read and write
- 5: Read and execute
- 4: Read only
- 3: Write and execute
- 2: Write only
- 1: Execute only
- 0: No access

The chmod command also permits administrators to create SUID and SGID permissions. SUID stands for Set User ID and permits a file owner to specify that anybody who executes the file executes it with the permissions of the file owner. SGID stands for Set Group ID and does the same thing, but the executing user uses the context of the possessing group. Both settings have some security risks involved, because both permissions grant special superuser privileges.

umask Value	File Permissions	Directory Permissions
077	- r w - - - - - - -	d r w x - - - - - -
027	- r w - r - - - - -	d r w x r - x - - -
007	- r w - r w - - - - -	d r w x r w x - - -
022	- r w - r - - r - -	d r w x r - x r - x
002	- r w - r w - r - -	d r w x r w x r - x

Table 3-4   These are some common umask values and their associated permissions

The default permissions created on a file and time of the creation depend on the umask value. The umask command assesses the default access assigned to files and directories. The command is executed whenever the system starts up or other users log into the system. The umask value is originally an output of an XOR operation and the values vary from those summarized with the chmod command. Table 3-4 shows some common umask values.

System Log Utility (Syslog)

The System Log (syslog) utility enables numerous system utilities to log events, errors, and data using the same approach. This way, each utility does not have to execute its own logging utility. Syslog can record messages from Linux applications and tools, such as Web servers and e-mail programs. From a security point of view, syslog also allows organizations to maintain logs on a separate system. This helps in hiding the logs from intruders who can compromise the system.

Syslog is capable of delivering log information from a sender to a receiver across an IP network. Syslog messages are sent via UDP and/or TCP. It is supported by a wide variety of devices and receivers of different platforms, so syslog is used to integrate log data from different types of systems to a central repository.

Syslog text is no more than 1,024 bytes in length. Syslog messages are received on UDP port 514. The machines or devices receiving these syslog messages are called syslog servers or syslog domains. Because the syslog protocol is UDP based, it cannot guarantee the delivery of messages. Also, the receiver of the syslog messages cannot be certain that the message is from the reported server.

UNIX Security Checklist

- Do not attach the machine to an insecure network until all security steps have been addressed. If possible, perform all installations on the machine while it is completely isolated from any network. This may be facilitated by the use of patches stored on a CD or file server located within an isolated staging network.

- Retrieve the latest patch list from the vendor and retrieve any recommended security patches not included with the system. Some patches may reenable default configurations so it is important to go through this checklist after installing any new patches or packages. Patches for software applications not supplied by the operating system vendor should be obtained directly from the software vendor's Web site.

- Ensure that software patches and packages are downloaded only from a reliable source, such as direct from the vendor or a trusted mirror. This also applies to the operating system if it is publicly available or open source.

- Verify the cryptographic digital signature of any signed downloaded files to ensure integrity. Do not use a file whose signature does not match its contents.

- Verify the MD5 checksum of any downloaded patches with a utility such as md5 or md5sum.

- Subscribe to the vendor's security update mailing list.

- Subscribe to security advisory mailing lists from the local incident response team. These mailing lists are typically low volume and provide invaluable information for system and security administrators.

Macintosh Security

There are many features that harden the security of the Macintosh OS, including:

- Secure default configuration
- Personal firewall
- FileVault
- Secure keychain
- Permanent deletion
- Disk image encryption

Using Kerberos Authentication

Kerberos is an authentication protocol that provides the facility to authenticate the client and server with the help of third-party authentication. It is mainly used to provide authentication for services such as telnet and e-mail. With this protocol, the client can trust the server without a username and password.

Kerberos authentication can be used in Mac OS X; the login window can be configured to require Kerberos authentication. To enable Kerberos authentication, an administrator can edit the /etc/authorization file. This can only be done with root privileges.

First, the administrator must locate the following code in the file:

```
<key>system.login.console</key>

<dict>

<key>eval</key>\

-><string>loginwindow_builtin:login,authinternal,loginwindow_builtin:\

->succedd</string>
```

He or she then changes it to the following:

```
<key>system.login.console</key>

<dict>

<key>eval</key>\

-><string>loginwindow_builtin:login,krb5auth:authoverify,\

->loginwindow_bultin:success</string>
```

Rendezvous Security

There are some security concerns with using Rendezvous. For example, if a Mac OS X host fails to make contact or link with its primary DNS server, a multicast DNS request is sent for the address. If an attacker wants to intrude, he or she can respond with a malicious DNS address.

Applications running on the same host should make a distinction between the two hostnames acquired through normal DNS and those acquired through Rendezvous. The global names that have Rendezvous hostnames should be considered highly suspicious. Like Safari, Apple Browser can show a Web site discovered through Rendezvous in its own pane.

Rendezvous services are less secure when they are discovered through normal routes. Multicast DNS–Service Discovery (mDNS-SD) is inherently distributed, rather than centralized like traditional DNS, and is the only mechanism to find services such as P2P and iTunes. Every device advertises the service it provides by sending a multicast notification message that describes the type of the service and provides the name, IP address, port, and other information.

Restricting User Capabilities

Mac OS X has reintroduced admin user control over the local users through capabilities, a function of the account preference pane. In Mac OS X 10.3, capabilities are renamed limitations and in Mac OS X 10.4, they are renamed parental controls.

Argument	Result
-R	Recursively descends through directory arguments to change the user ID and/or group ID.
-H	If -R is specified, symbolic links on the command line are followed. Symbolic links encountered in tree traversal are not followed.
-L	If -R is specified, all symbolic links are followed.
-P	If -R is specified, no symbolic links are followed.
-f	Forces an attempt to change user ID and/or group ID without reporting any errors.
-h	If the file is a symbolic link, the user ID and/or group ID of the link is changed.

Table 3-5 These arguments can be used with chown

With the help of these, a user can allow or deny non-admin users the ability to:

- Open all system preference panes
- Burn discs
- Change password
- Use the simple Finder
- Open individual applications and remove items from the dock

To set user capabilities, a user can follow these steps:

1. Open System preferences.
2. Choose **Account** from the **View** menu.
3. Select any non-admin user.
4. Click **Capabilities, Limitations,** or **Parental controls.**
5. Check the check boxes as desired.
6. Click **OK.**

All of these features can only be set for non-admin users.

Command-Line Administration Tools

For the maintenance and configuration of user accounts, a number of command-line administration tools are available, including:

- NetInfo Utilities
- The nidump, niutil, and niload commands for account creation and deletion
- The common BSD tools

To change the ownership of a file, the chown command is used. This command can be executed by root users.

Table 3-5 shows the arguments than can be used with chown and their results.

Upgrading to Windows Vista

Windows Vista has many security features, including the following:

- With the help of user account controls, a user can change common settings. Administrative privileges are not required. This prevents users from making potentially dangerous changes to their computers, without limiting their ability to run applications.
- The built-in Web browser in Windows Vista, Microsoft Internet Explorer, has many security enhancements, such as a phishing filter and protection from spoofing attacks. A protected mode is added to Internet Explorer to protect user data and configuration settings from being deleted or modified by malicious Web sites or malware.

- Windows Defender detects many types of potentially suspicious software and can prompt the user before allowing applications to make potentially malicious changes.

- The new outbound filtering in the firewall provides administrative control over peer-to-peer sharing applications and similar applications that businesses want to restrict.

- Windows Service Hardening limits the damage attackers can do in the unlikely event that they are able to successfully compromise a service. As a result, the risk of attackers making permanent changes to the Windows Vista client or attacking other computers on the network is reduced.

- Administrators can use Network Access Protection to prevent clients that do not meet the internal system health policy from connecting to the internal network and potentially spreading malware to other machines.

Installing Windows Vista

To perform a clean installation of Windows Vista, there are two methods that can be followed. The following method involves running the setup program after starting the computer in its current operating system:

1. Start the computer in its current operating system.

2. Insert the Windows Vista DVD in the computer's DVD drive.

3. If Windows automatically detects the DVD, the **Install** screen appears. Click **Install now.** If it does not automatically detect the DVD, follow these steps:

   a. Click **Start**, click **Run**, type **<Drive>:\setup.exe,** and then click the OK button. *<Drive>* is the drive letter of the computer's DVD drive.

   b. Click Insta**ll now.**

4. When the **Which type of installation do you want?** screen appears, click **Custom (advanced),** and then follow the instructions that are displayed on the screen to install Windows Vista.

The following method involves booting the Windows Vista DVD directly:

1. Start the computer by using the Windows Vista DVD. To do this, insert the Windows Vista DVD in the computer's DVD drive and then restart the computer. To start the computer from the Windows Vista DVD, the computer must be configured to start from the DVD drive.

2. When the **Press any key to boot from CD** message is displayed on the screen, press a key.

3. Follow the instructions that are displayed on the screen to install Windows Vista.

Chapter Summary

- The BIOS should be patched to make sure it is always the current version.

- The Windows registry is a centralized storage area in Windows, containing details of system configuration, devices, applications, user accounts, and ports.

- All local users and user groups are handled by the WinLogon process.

- LSA calls the NetLogon process if the user is using a domain account.

- A Discretionary Access Control List (DACL) is a list of user accounts and group accounts that have authorization to use an object.

- Active Directory is a collection of security information, such as certificates and crypto keys, distributed between domain controllers. This includes user accounts, system accounts, and administrative information of a network.

- Kerberos is a Windows and UNIX authentication protocol to check the authenticity of client and server computers in an open network.

- The Linux file system is organized as a tree structure, storing all files with their location addresses in a hierarchical format.

- Data security in Linux is achieved using several mechanisms, including encryption, integrity checks, and digital signatures.
- Pluggable Authentication Module (PAM) is a series of library modules that depend on configuration files for authentication of system users.
- The System Log (syslog) utility enables numerous system utilities to log events, errors, and data using the same approach. That way, each utility does not have to execute its own logging utility.

Review Questions

1. What are the benefits of EFS?

   _____

   _____

   _____

   _____

2. What are the security services of Windows network security?

   _____

   _____

   _____

   _____

3. Why is a centralized database used in the Active Directory?

   _____

   _____

   _____

   _____

4. What are user configuration policies?

   _____

   _____

   _____

   _____

5. What is a directory services agent?

   _____

   _____

   _____

   _____

6. What is a Kerberos ticket?

   _____

   _____

   _____

   _____

7. What are manual secret keys?

_____

_____

_____

_____

8. What are Group Policy Management Console facilities?

_____

_____

_____

_____

9. How is a file encrypted for multiple users?

_____

_____

_____

_____

10. What are the steps to import a CA certificate from Microsoft Certificate Services?

_____

_____

_____

_____

11. What are the different run levels for Linux services?

_____

_____

_____

_____

12. What is the ls command?

_____

_____

_____

_____

13. What is the chmod command?

_____

_____

_____

_____

14. What is PAM?

_____

_____

_____

_____

Hands-On Projects

1. Use Rootkit Revealer to detect rootkits.

   ▪ Navigate to Chapter 3 of the Student Resource Center.

   ▪ Install and launch the RootkitRevealer program.

   ▪ To hide the standard NTFS metadata files, click **Options** and select **Hide standard NTFS Metadata files**.

   ▪ Choose **Options** and select **Scan Registry** to scan the registry.

   ▪ To perform a scan, click **File** and select **Scan**.

   ▪ If any rootkits are found, they will be shown, as seen in Figure 3-7.

Figure 3-7 RootkitRevealer will show any rootkits installed in a Windows system.

- Click **Abort** to stop scanning.
- To save the scan result, choose **File** and then **Save**.
- To exit the RootkitRevealer application, choose **File** and then **Exit**.

2. Use Unlocker to delete files or folders when access is denied.

- Navigate to Chapter 3 of the Student Resource Center.
- Install and launch the Unlocker program.
- Right-click the file or folder to be deleted. Click **Unlocker**.
- Click the action to be performed on the folder by selecting an option from the drop-down menu, as shown in Figure 3-8.

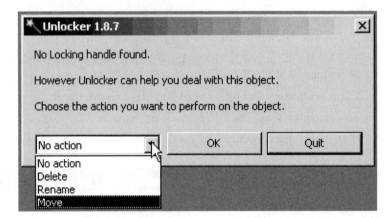

Figure 3-8   Unlocker will perform the selected action on files or folders when access is denied.

Chapter 4

Patch Management

Objectives

After completing this chapter, you should be able to:

- Understand patch management
- Test patches
- Understand patch monitoring and management
- Identify and install patches on Red Hat networks
- Implement Windows Update services
- Work with patch management tools

Key Terms

Production computer   a system configured to run business applications and services

Test computer   a system used exclusively for testing new software

Introduction to Patch Management

Patch management is a process that ensures that the appropriate patches are installed on systems. This helps to maintain operational efficiency and effectiveness, overcome security vulnerabilities, and maintain system stability. This chapter helps you understand how to manage patches for Linux and Windows systems in order to minimize known vulnerabilities.

Patching

Patching is used to correct software deficiencies and update systems with new features. Patch management involves the following:

- Choosing, verifying, testing, and applying patches
- Updating previously applied patches with current patches

- Listing patches applied previously to current software
- Recording repositories, or depots, of patches for easy selection
- Assigning and deploying applied patches

The following are some of the potential consequences for failing to apply the necessary patches:

- Downtime and remediation time
- Loss of data integrity
- Loss of credibility
- Negative public relations
- Legal issues
- Stolen intellectual property

Applying Updates

Updates are required to be made frequently due to functional changes and newly discovered security problems. These updates may be available on the Internet or may come bundled with products.

Updating Red Hat Software

Red Hat provides the up2date update tool that automatically patches and installs the latest available software from the Red Hat network Web site. Red Hat Linux can be updated either through the graphical user interface or through the command line.

Change Management Rules

Updating or making changes to currently installed software may incur several negative consequences if not properly managed. Making a large change can be very difficult for any organization, because all the processes and functionalities running on the network are affected. To reduce these negative effects, every organization must follow a change management process. While creating this process, the following points must be considered:

- The change must be as uncomplicated as possible.
- The effect of change must be appropriate to the level of change.
- Management must support the change by enforcing it.
- Company culture must adapt to change management.
- Change management policy must be properly documented.
- Changes must be aligned to the business objectives.
- The effects of patches must be carefully monitored.

Microsoft Software Fixes

Microsoft periodically releases software updates to correct issues or vulnerabilities that are revealed after a product has been released. When Microsoft is made aware of a security vulnerability, the issue is appraised and confirmed by the Microsoft Security Response Center (MSRC) and the appropriate product groups. The product groups then test the issues and create a security update to remedy the issue. The MSRC team works with the reporter of the vulnerability to organize the public release of the security update. Microsoft then distributes the new security update through the Microsoft Download Center and other services, including the following:

- Automatic Updates:
  - Microsoft Windows Update
  - Microsoft Office Update
  - Microsoft Update
- User Initiated Updates:
  - Microsoft Systems Management Server (SMS) 2003

- Microsoft Windows Server Update Service (WSUS)
- Microsoft System Center Configuration Manager 2007 (SCCM)

Types of Patches Defined by Microsoft

Microsoft releases patches that update the Windows OS and other Microsoft applications. These patches have three levels, depending on their size and scope:

1. *Hotfixes*: Hotfixes are updates that deal with a single newly discovered problem. They are created and released quickly, with less testing compared to other updates. Some hotfixes are referred to as security fixes, because they deal with issues identified by the Microsoft Security Response Center (MSRC), rather than by Microsoft Product Support Services (MPSS). These are also referred to as Quick Fix Engineering (QFE) fixes.

2. *Rollups*: Rollup fixes combine the updates of several hotfixes into a single update file. These have undergone many tests but are released more frequently than service packs.

3. *Service packs*: Service packs go through extensive testing before release to minimize deployment issues. Microsoft might issue several beta releases of a service pack before notifying the public.

When a security fix is released, MSRC issues a security bulletin that identifies the addressed vulnerability. A severity rating is also applied to the security bulletin. In the case of a rollup fix, the highest security rating of the individual hotfixes in the rollup is applied.

The ratings based on MSRC terms are:

- *Critical*: This fixes a vulnerability that permits the propagation of an Internet worm without user action. Administrators should apply critical updates as soon as possible after testing.

- *Important*: This fixes a vulnerability that compromises the confidentiality, integrity, or availability of user data, and the integrity or availability of processing resources. Administrators should apply important updates as soon as possible after testing.

- *Moderate*: This rating is applied to vulnerabilities that can be avoided. Before testing and deploying them, administrators should determine if they are necessary for the specific system.

- *Low*: Low-rated patches fix vulnerabilities that are difficult to exploit or whose impact is minimal. Before testing and deploying them, administrators should determine if they are necessary for the specific system.

Patch Testing

The first step in patch testing is to verify the patch source and integrity, in order to ensure that the update is valid and unaltered. This can be done by checking digital signatures and/or checksums. The patch testing process takes place in three different categories: installation, applications, and services.

There are two types of computers in patch testing. A ***production computer*** is a desktop or server system configured to run business applications and services. A ***test computer***, on the other hand, is used exclusively for testing new software.

Testing Patch Installation

It is important to know the scope of a patch before testing a patch installation. When testing a patch, an administrator should list the update packages that are required. If there are any dependent packages, he or she should include them in testing.

Testing Application Patches

Application patches may provide security improvements, additional features, and bug fixes. When testing application patches, an administrator should follow these steps:

1. If there are any configuration files related to an application, back up those files.

2. Test the application patch carefully. Install it on the test system and list the files that are downloaded.

3. Test the patch on the test system.

4. Identify the changes to the file configuration.

5. If there are any problems with the patch, reevaluate if the patch is necessary.

6. Before installing the patch on the production computer, notify the users who will be affected.

Testing Service Patches

Testing a service patch may improve the security of the system, provide additional features, and fix bugs. When testing a service patch, an administrator should follow these steps:

1. If there are any configuration files related to an application, back up those files.

2. Test the service patch carefully. Install it in on the test system and list the files that are downloaded.

3. Test the patch on the test system.

4. Identify the differences from previous configuration files.

5. If the services of the system are shared on a network, test the upgrades from another system.

6. If there are any problems with the patch, reevaluate if the patch is necessary.

7. Before installing the patch on the production computer, notify the users who will be affected.

Patch Management and Monitoring

Patch management includes the following steps:

1. Identify the patch location by understanding the following concepts:
   - Baseline of system security
   - Constantly reviewing the patch management architecture
   - Managing SMS client breadth and health
   - Conducting inventories

2. Identify new patches and verify patch authenticity by installing each patch on a test computer.

3. Ensure that both patch testing and risk assessment are done at one place.

4. Deploying the patch includes the following:
   - Patch installation
   - Patch distribution
   - Patch monitoring
   - Patch reporting

Identifying and Installing Patches on Red Hat Networks

Patching a Linux operating system is a straightforward process. Downloading a regular patch is not a problem for a typical Internet connection, but it can be an issue to download the same patch for many computers on the network. To avoid this, administrators should implement a central patch management process and configure it. This can be done with the help of Red Hat Enterprise Linux (RHEL). To administer a patch management process over RHEL, administrators can set up a Red Hat proxy server that will manage the patch process.

Configuring the Proxy Server

A proxy server is a server program that serves the requests of its clients by making requests to other servers on that network. The steps to configure a proxy server from the command line are as follows:

1. Install RHEL with the minimal configuration to support networking.

2. Configure the firewall to allow communication with the Red Hat Network.

3. Set up a connection to a Network Time Protocol (NTP) server.

4. Configure the RHEL computer as a router.

5. Register this RHEL computer on the Red Hat Network.

6. Download proxy packages over a Red Hat network channel.

7. Install the proxy server packages.

8. Through proxy subscription, monitor this RHEL computer.

9. Configure the proxy server.

10. In order for clients to communicate with the proxy server, create certification keys.

After completion of this process, the administrator should configure the clients on the network and gather updates from this RHEL computer.

Configuring the Proxy Client

Configuration of the proxy client is a straightforward process. The administrator has to reconfigure the update agent to take updates from the proxy server rather than from the Red Hat Network. He or she must gather the certificate keys from the proxy server installation process. Through RHEL clients, the process can be automated with scripts.

Red Hat Up2date Patch Management Utility

To install patches using up2date, an administrator can follow these steps:

1. Double-click the exclamation mark in the lower-right side of the screen, or open a console window and type **up2date**.

2. Read the **Terms of Service** window and click **Forward**.

3. The **Proxy Configuration** screen will appear. Click **Forward**.

4. The **Configuration Complete** window will appear. Click **Apply**.

5. If the system has not yet been registered, then a warning window will appear. Double-click the **RHN Tool** indicator or type **up2date** in a shell window.

6. Provide the root login.

7. The **Red Hat Network Configuration** window will appear to provide special configuration options.

8. Red Hat provides a GPG key to verify that the downloaded files are genuine. Click **Yes** to import and continue.

9. Double-click the icon in the bottom right of the screen or type **up2date** to bring up the **Red Hat Update Agent** welcome screen. Click **Forward** and fill in the login information in the **Red Hat Network login** window. Then click **Forward** once again.

10. The **Hardware Profile** window will take the initial update configuration information to register the system with the Red Hat Network. This step should be skipped to maintain privacy. Click **Forward** in the **Send Profile Information to Red Hat Network** screen.

11. The system will now collect specific information regarding the software installed. This information allows Red Hat to customize the list of updates.

12. After the registration is finished, updating can start. Double-click the **RHN Update** icon or type **up2date** on the command line. Click **Forward**.

13. The **Channel** window will appear, giving a list of Red Hat channels with descriptions.

14. The **Package List** window will appear, listing all the available packages that can be updated by the Red Hat Network. After selecting packages, click **Forward**.

15. The system will resolve any interdependencies or conflicts. After this, all packages that were selected will be downloaded from Red Hat.

16. After packages are retrieved, the installation process will begin.

17. After packages are successfully installed, a list of changes will appear.

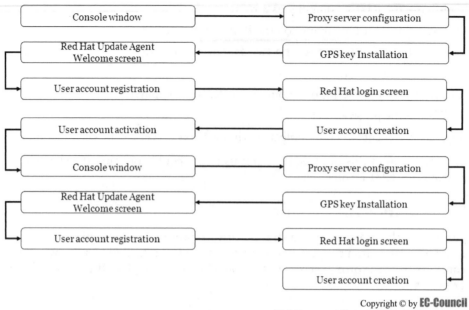

Figure 4-1   This flowchart shows the up2date patch management process.

Figure 4-1 shows a flowchart of this process.

Up2date Command-Line Interface

Up2date can be executed from the command line using the following syntax:

```
up2date --configure --d --dry-run -f -i -l --nox --showall -u
```

Table 4-1 describes the options of this command-line tool.

Option	Description
--configure	Configure the up2date agent
--d	Download packages for future installation
--dry-run	Show available packages and dependencies
-f	Force package installation
-i	Begin installation
-l	List updated, downloaded, and installed packages
--nox	Do not display the GUI
--showall	Show all available packages
-u	Update all currently installed packages

Table 4-1   These are the options for up2date's command-line interface

Security Patch Compliance

Security patch compliance provides up-to-date security for patch management. Scanning will take place for all managed systems on a regular basis to identify missing patches. This provides a report for vulnerabilities addressed by the missing patch and gives the status of patch deployment.

Distribution

The following are the steps to distribute a patch:

1. Use the **Navigate** panel to expand **Software Management**.
2. Click **Distribute** and press **Patches**.
3. Look for the task name field and type the name of the task.
4. In the **Select Software** section, click the **Patches** option.
5. Use **Views** and **Types** to search for the particular patch name or click **Advanced** for more options, and then select the appropriate item.
6. Specify the order to distribute the patches from selected software tables using the arrow keys.
7. Select the **Computer** section.
8. Use **Views** and **Types** to search for a particular target name, or click **Advanced** for more options.
9. Select the appropriate items from the search results.
10. Specify the time and date to distribute the patches in the **Schedule** section.
11. In the **Notification** section, specify the status of the patch distribution to host machines.
12. Click the **Submit** button to distribute the patches.

Troubleshoot Security Patch Management

Troubleshooting is a process of identifying problems in security patch management and fixing them using troubleshooting tools.

Reporting

Reporting mainly contains the details of patch installations, patch distributions, and progress reports that give the status of the entire project. Reporting mainly covers:

- Update status
- Computer status
- Computer compliance status
- Update compliance status
- Synchronization (or download) status

Microsoft Patch Management Process

Microsoft recommends a six-step process for patch management. This process ensures that patches are applied in a structured way, and keeps other applications on the network from failing. These six steps are:

1. *Identification*: New security updates or service packs must be identified to ensure that they are installed in a timely manner.
2. *Assessment*: It should be determined if updates are necessary to be installed.
3. *Obtainment*: Obtain the security update or service pack installation files from Microsoft.
4. *Testing*: Perform tests on the security updates or service packs prior to implementation to ensure that they will not cause undesired side effects.
5. *Deployment*: Use tools to organize the software updates.
6. *Confirmation*: Ensure that software updates were successfully installed.

Identification

The first step in patch management is responding quickly when Microsoft releases security patches. When a security patch is released, Microsoft issues a security bulletin that details the vulnerability the security patch fixes and its vulnerability rating. The notification service sends an e-mail when a new security bulletin is released. Microsoft also releases information about security patches through Windows Live Alerts and RSS feeds. In addition to the Microsoft Security Notification Service, it may be wise to subscribe to NTBugtraq (*http://www.ntbugtraq.com*) and the Computer Emergency Response Team (CERT) Advisory Mailing List (*http://www.cert.org/contact_cert/certmaillist.html*).

Assessment

When a security patch is identified, administrators must determine whether the vulnerability affects the company and whether the organization's computers require the patch. Microsoft security bulletin rating systems can help administrators make that decision.

Administrators must keep an inventory of the organization's systems to help in planning patch deployment. They can then segregate the computers by identifying which computers are affected by the vulnerability. For example, if Microsoft releases a new security bulletin relating to a bug in Microsoft Exchange 2008 Server, it is useful to know how many instances of Exchange 2008 Server are on the network.

By utilizing software such as Microsoft's Systems Management Server (SMS), administrators can establish a detailed inventory of network computers. This inventory information determines which service packs and hotfixes are applied to which computer. Computers are classified into collections depending on the inventory for deploying service packs and hotfixes. For example, creating a collection of all Windows 2003–based computers helps in the deployment of the latest Windows 2003 service pack.

Inventory

Applications that are chosen for an inventory mechanism must be able to answer the following questions:

- What versions of the OS are in use?
- How many OSs need to be patched?
- How many application versions and applications are in use?
- Do different applications or different OSs need different patches?
- How many unpatched systems are being used?
- How many unmanaged systems are being used?
- Which systems are mission critical?
- How is the patch distributed for existing software dependencies?

Baselining

When establishing baselines, administrators must keep these points in mind:

- Identify the baseline computers and match them with their compliances. Discuss issues such as the distribution, schedules, permissions, and exception handlings that may exist with these computers.
- Check for unauthorized changes to computers that exceed their class baseline.
- Identify the systems that have exemptions from the baseline due to special circumstances. It is advised not to upgrade baselines to such systems because of their approved applications.
- Use technologies like Microsoft Baseline Security Analyzer (MBSA), New Boundary's Prism Patch Manager, or Shavlik's HFNetCheck for scanning the baseline systems to avoid false positives. These technologies are discussed later.

Obtainment

After identifying the computers that are to be patched, the administrator must obtain the patches or service pack files. The method and location for obtaining the files depends on several factors, including which application or OS is affected by the patch, whether all network computers are connected to the Internet, and whether a service pack or hotfix deployment solution is available.

The following locations are available for downloading service packs and hotfixes:

- Microsoft Windows Update
- Microsoft Office Product Updates
- Microsoft Download Center

Windows Update

Windows Update is the online extension of Windows that helps keep computers up to date. Windows Update supports Windows 98, Windows Millennium Edition, Windows 2000, Windows XP, Windows Vista, and Windows Server 2003. Customers can use Windows Update to choose updates for a computer's operating system software and hardware drivers. New content is added to Windows Update as soon as new updates for Windows are available from Microsoft, making this tool the authoritative source for the latest updates to the Windows operating systems listed above.

To use the Windows Update site, the following requirements must be met:

- Microsoft Internet Explorer must have cookies enabled. The Windows Update site uses cookies to detect and record security patch installation data. Windows Update recognizes a computer by creating a globally unique identifier (GUID), which is stored in a cookie. The cookie contains the following information to recognize a computer:

  - The OS version for determining security patches related to the OS and service pack level

  - The Internet Explorer version for determining Internet Explorer version-specific updates

  - The version number for other software that can be updated by Windows Update, including Windows Media Player and Microsoft SQL Server

  - The Plug and Play identification numbers of hardware devices to determine required hardware device driver updates

  - The region and language settings to determine whether a localized version of a security patch must be installed

- Internet Explorer must allow Microsoft ActiveX controls. The Windows Update site downloads an ActiveX control to determine which security patches are required by the target computer. To enable the download of the ActiveX control, the security settings for the Internet zone in Internet Explorer must be set to medium or lower.

- The person running the ActiveX control must be a member of the local administrators group. Only members of the local administrators group have the necessary permissions to scan the file system and registry to determine whether a security update is installed. In addition, only members of the local administrators group have the necessary permissions to install security updates.

Using Windows Update is a simple three-step process:

1. Enter Windows Update and click **Scan for Updates**.

2. Browse through the available updates in each category, and then click **Add** to select an update and add it to the collection of updates to install. If necessary, read a full description of each item by clicking the **Read More** link.

3. When all required updates are selected, click **Review and Install Updates**, and then click **Install Now**.

Microsoft Office Product Updates

Office Update is similar in concept to Windows Update; however, it is restricted to updates for the Microsoft Office product suite. Users visit the Office Update site and select **Check for Updates** to trigger a scan of a computer's Microsoft Office installation for missing software updates or service packs. A detailed list of the missing updates needed to bring the system up to date is displayed, and the selected updates are then installed on the computer.

Microsoft Download Center

The Microsoft Download Center allows users to search for software and updates from Microsoft. Users must manually designate a download location. The following update categories are available from the Microsoft Download Center:

- *Games*: Trial versions and updates for games from Microsoft

- *Microsoft DirectX*: Updates and the latest versions of DirectX

- *Internet*: Updates for all Internet-based applications, such as Windows Messenger and Internet Explorer

- *Windows (security and updates)*: Security updates for any component of Windows

- *Windows Media*: Updates and codecs for Windows Media Player
- *Drivers*: Updated drivers for Microsoft hardware and updates for common OS components, such as Microsoft Data Access Components (MDAC)
- *Office and Home Applications*: Updates for Microsoft Office and other home applications, such as Microsoft MapPoint
- *Mobile Devices*: Updates for the Palm PC, Microsoft ActiveSync, and Windows CE
- *Macintosh and Other Platforms*: Updates of software for Macintosh, Solaris, and UNIX computers
- *Server Applications*: Updates for Microsoft BackOffice components, such as Microsoft SQL Server, Microsoft Exchange Server, Microsoft Systems Management Server (SMS), and Microsoft SharePoint Portal Server
- *System Management Tools*: Updates for Windows management, including Windows Installer, the Internet Information Services (IIS) Lockdown Tool, and Sysprep
- *Development Resources*: Updates for Microsoft Visual Basic, the Microsoft .NET Framework, and Microsoft Visual Studio

Testing

In an enterprise network, it is risky to deploy service packs or hotfixes without testing in the system environment. Testing guarantees that the application of a service pack or hotfix does not create any undesired side effects.

One option to ensure that the testing is valid is to deploy a test network. A test network contains computers with the standard configuration used on the network. Another option is to implement a pilot project, where patches are tested by a subset of network computers. Either of these options will guarantee that a patch does not have issues with other applications installed on a standard desktop computer.

Once initial testing is completed, deployment of the patch can begin.

Deployment

To install service packs for Windows, an administrator should follow these steps:

1. In Internet Explorer, go to *http://technet.microsoft.com/*, find the latest service packs for the target system, and click the link for the most recent service pack.
2. If necessary, select the language matching the system to be updated and click **Change**.
3. Click the **Download** link. Internet Explorer will show a prompt asking whether to save the installation file or run it immediately.
4. Choose to either install the service pack immediately or save the installation file.
5. If the file is saved, double-click on the file to install the service pack.

Other Methods of Installing Service Packs

Service packs can also be installed through Windows Update. Windows Update can be configured to automatically download service pack updates. Administrators can then install the service packs by accessing Windows Update through the Windows Control Panel.

Deployment Preparation

The steps required to prepare the software update for deployment include:

- Communicating the rollout schedule to all affected employees
- Deploying Software Update Services (SUS)
  - Gathering updates for the SUS server
- Deploying the System Management Server (SMS)
  - Importing the programs from test environments and advertising them
  - Assigning distribution points

- Gathering the updates using distribution points
- Selecting the distribution points

Deployment of the Patch

The process of deploying a patch mainly depends on the type and nature of the patch. The steps required to deploy a patch or software update include:

1. Advertising the software update on the client systems
2. Monitoring and reporting the status of deployment
3. Handling failed deployments

Confirmation

After hotfix installation, administrators must make sure that it is installed successfully. Several methods are available to determine whether a hotfix is correctly applied, including the following:

- *Inspect the file system*: When a hotfix is installed and the replaced files are archived, the archived files are stored in the %windir%\$NTUninstallQ######$ folder, where ###### refers to the related Microsoft Knowledge Base article number. If the folder exists, the hotfix was applied correctly. This does not, however, prevent the updated version from being replaced by an incorrect version at a later time, especially with hotfixes released prior to Service Pack 3 of Windows 2000 that do not have QChain.exe functionality.

- *Inspect the registry*: When a hotfix is installed, the installation program registers the hotfix in the *HKLM\Software\Microsoft\Windows NT\CurrentVersion\Hotfix\Q######* registry key, where ###### is the related Microsoft Knowledge Base article. Again, this does not prevent the update from being replaced with an incorrect version later.

- *Use hotfix diagnosis tools*: There are several available hotfix diagnosis tools, including the Microsoft Baseline Security Analyzer command-line version executable Mbsacli.exe, Shavlik's hotfix network checker HfNetChk.exe, and those found on the Microsoft Windows Update Web site. Such tools determine whether the hotfix needs reapplication by inspecting the checksums on the updated files.

Implementing Windows Update Services

In order to maintain the security of a network, it is essential to keep the operating system patched regularly. Over time, Microsoft has addressed this issue by implementing software update services such as the Microsoft Software Update Services (SUS), Windows Server Update Services (WSUS), Microsoft Systems Management Server (SMS), and System Center Configuration Manager (SCCM).

Microsoft Software Update Services (SUS)

Windows 2000 and Windows Server 2000 are provided with an add-in component called Microsoft Software Update Services (SUS). SUS enables the installation of updates from the Internet on desktops and servers. The updates can be scheduled synchronously on the SUS server. Once the updates are downloaded to the server, the SUS server can install them on the client on request.

Windows Server Update Services (WSUS)

Windows Server Update Services is the name of the latest version of Software Update Services (SUS). WSUS is a patch management and update component, and offers a solution for the software distribution and update management infrastructure. WSUS is divided into two components: the client and server.

The WSUS client runs on the following components:

- Windows 2000 Service Pack 3 (SP3) and later
- Windows XP and later
- Windows Server 2003

The WSUS server runs on the following components:

- Windows 2000 Service Pack 4 (SP4) and later
- Windows Server 2003

WSUS has replaced SMS in organizations that depend on open source and effortless deployments. WSUS also supports service packs.

Server-Side Features of WSUS

- Timely updates along with product support for Windows, Office, Exchange Server, and SQL Server.
- Targeting capabilities that facilitate the deployment of updates to a single system or a group of systems. The configuration can be done on the WSUS server directly or through group policy in Active Directory. It can also be achieved on the client system by editing registry settings.

Client-Side Features of WSUS

- Powerful and flexible management of the Automatic Updates service.
- Group policies are useful for configuring the behavior of Automatic Updates. Automatic Updates can also be configured remotely with the help of registry keys and a logon script.
- Self-updating is available for client computers.
- The client computers when connected to a WSUS server can automatically detect the Automatic Updates available and subsequently can install the Automatic Updates automatically.

Installation Steps

The following are the steps for installing WSUS:

- *Step 1*: Confirm WSUS installation requirements.
- *Step 2*: Install WSUS Server or Administration Console.
- *Step 3*: Configure the network connections.
- *Step 4*: Configure updates and synchronization.
- *Step 5*: Configure client updates.
- *Step 6*: Configure computer groups.
- *Step 7*: Approve and deploy WSUS updates.

Step 1: Confirm WSUS Installation Requirements The following permissions are required for the specified users and directories:

- The NT Authority\Network Service account must have Full Control permission for the following folders so that the WSUS Administration snap-in displays correctly:
  - %windir%\Microsoft .NET\Framework\v2.0.50727\Temporary ASP.NET Files
  - %windir%\Temp
- The account used to install WSUS must be a member of the Local Administrators group.

If the machine is running Windows 7 or Windows Server 2008 SP2, the administrator can install WSUS from Server Manager. If the machine is running another supported operating system or the administrator is installing only the WSUS Administration Console, he or she can install WSUS by using the WSUSSetup.exe file.

The following are the steps to prepare to install WSUS Server by using Server Manager:

1. Log on to the server on which you plan to install WSUS using an account that is a member of the Local Administrators group.

2. Click **Start**, point to **Administrative Tools**, and then click **Server Manager**.

3. In the right pane of the **Server Manager** window, in the **Roles Summary** section, click **Add Roles**.

4. If the **Before You Begin** page appears, click **Next**.

5. On the **Select Server Roles** page, confirm that **Application Server and Web Server (IIS)** are selected. If they have been selected, use the remainder of this step to confirm that the required role services are selected. Otherwise, install Application Server and Web Server (IIS) as follows:

   - On the **Select Server Roles** page, select **Application Server and Web Server (IIS)**. Click **Next**.

   - If you are installing Application Role Services, on the **Application Server** page, click **Next**. On the **Application Server Role Services** page, choose the settings, and then click **Next**.

   - If you are installing Web Server IIS, on the **Web Server (IIS)** page, click **Next**. On the **Web Server (IIS) Role Services** page, in addition to the default settings, select **ASP.NET, Windows Authentication, Dynamic Content Compression,** and **IIS 6 Management Compatibility**. If the **Add Roles Wizard** window appears, click **Add Required Role Services**. Click **Next**.

   - On the **Confirm Installation Selections** page, click **Install**.

   - On the **Installation Results** page, confirm that an "Installation succeeded" message appears for the role services that you installed in this step, and then click **Close**.

Step 2: Install WSUS Server or Administration Console The following are the steps to install WSUS Server by using Server Manager:

1. Log on to the server on which you plan to install WSUS using an account that is a member of the Local Administrators group.

2. Click **Start**, point to **Administrative Tools**, and then click **Server Manager**.

3. In the right pane of the **Server Manager** window, in the **Roles Summary** section, click **Add Roles**.

4. If the **Before You Begin** page appears, click **Next**.

5. On the **Select Server Roles** page, select **Windows Server Update Services**.

6. On the **Windows Server Update Services** page, click **Next**.

7. On the **Confirm Installation Selections** page, click **Install**.

8. When the WSUS Setup Wizard is started, continue installing WSUS.

The following are the steps to install WSUS Server or the WSUS Administration Console by using the WSUS-Setup.exe file:

1. Log on to the server on which you plan to install WSUS by using an account that is a member of the Local Administrators group.

2. Double-click the WSUSSetup.exe installer file.

3. The Windows Server Update Services Setup Wizard is started.

The following are the steps for installing WSUS using the WSUS Setup Wizard, which is launched from Server Manager or from the WSUSSetup.exe file:

1. On the **Welcome** page of the Windows Server Update Services Setup Wizard, click **Next**.

2. On the **Installation Mode Selection** page, select **Full server installation including Administration Console** if you want to install WSUS Server on this computer, or **Administration Console only** if you want to install the Administration Console only.

3. On the **License Agreement** page, read the terms of the license agreement, click **I accept the terms of the license agreement,** and then click **Next**.

4. You can specify where clients get updates on the **Select Update Source** page of the installation wizard. By default, the **Store updates locally** check box is selected and updates will be stored on the WSUS server in the location that you specify. If you clear the **Store updates locally** check box, client computers obtain approved updates by connecting to Microsoft Update. Make your selection, and then click **Next**.

5. On the **Database Options** page, select the software that is used to manage the WSUS database. By default, the installation wizard offers to install Windows Internal Database. If you do not want to use Windows Internal Database, provide an instance of Microsoft SQL Server for WSUS to use by selecting **Use an existing database on this server** or **Use an existing database server on a remote computer**. Type the instance name in the applicable box. The instance name should appear as <serverName>\<instanceName>, where

serverName is the name of the server and instanceName is the name of the SQL instance. Make your selection, and then click **Next**.

6. If you have opted to connect to a SQL Server, on the **Connecting to SQL Server Instance** page, WSUS will try to connect to the specified instance of SQL Server. When it has connected successfully, click **Next** to continue.

7. On the **Web Site Selection** page, specify the Web site that WSUS will use. If you want to use the default Web site on port 80, select **Use the existing IIS Default Web site**. If you already have a Web site on port 80, you can create an alternate site on port 8530 or 8531 by selecting **Create a Windows Server Update Services Web site**. Click **Next**.

8. On the **Ready to Install Windows Server Update Services** page, review the selections, and then click **Next**.

9. The final page of the installation wizard will let you know if the WSUS installation completed successfully. After you click **Finish**, the configuration wizard will start.

Step 3: Configure the Network Connections   This step involves the following procedures:

1. Configure your firewall. If there is a corporate firewall between WSUS and the Internet, you might have to configure that firewall to ensure WSUS can obtain updates. To obtain updates from Microsoft Update, the WSUS server uses port 80 for HTTP protocol and port 443 for HTTPS protocol.

2. Specify the way this server will obtain updates (either from Microsoft Update or from another WSUS server).

   - From the configuration wizard, after joining the Microsoft Improvement Program, click **Next** to select the upstream server.

   - If you choose to synchronize from Microsoft Update, you are finished with the **Options** page. Click **Next**, or select **Specify Proxy Server** from the navigation pane.

   - If you choose to synchronize from another WSUS server, specify the server name and the port on which this server will communicate with the upstream server.

   - To use SSL, select the **Use SSL when synchronizing update information** check box. In that case, the servers will use port 443 for synchronization. (Make sure that both this server and the upstream server support SSL.)

   - If this is a replica server, select the **This is a replica of the upstream server** check box. At this point, you are finished with upstream server configuration. Click **Next**, or select **Specify proxy server** from the left navigation pane.

3. Configure proxy server settings, so that WSUS can obtain updates.

   - On the **Specify Proxy Server** page of the configuration wizard, select the **Use a proxy server when synchronizing** check box, and then type the proxy server name and port number (port 80 by default) in the corresponding boxes.

   - If you want to connect to the proxy server by using specific user credentials, select the **Use user credentials to connect to the proxy server** check box, and then type the username, domain, and password of the user in the corresponding boxes. If you want to enable basic authentication for the user connecting to the proxy server, select the **Allow basic authentication (password is sent in cleartext)** check box.

   - At this point, you are finished with proxy server configuration. Click **Next** to go to the next page, where you can start to set up the synchronization process.

Step 4: Configure Updates and Synchronization   The following are the steps for configuring a set of updates to download using WSUS:

1. Save and download information about your upstream server and proxy server.

   - On the **Connect to Upstream Server** page of the configuration wizard, click the **Start Connecting** button. This both saves and uploads your settings and collects information about available updates.

   - While the connection is being made, the **Stop Connecting** button will be available. If there are problems with the connection, click **Stop Connecting**, fix the problems, and restart the connection.

   - After the download has completed successfully, click **Next**.

2. Choose the language of the updates.

   - The **Choose Languages** page lets you receive updates from all languages or from a subset of languages. Selecting a subset of languages will save disk space, but it is important to choose all of the languages that will be needed by all the clients of this WSUS server.

   - If you choose to get updates only for specific languages, select **Download updates only in these languages,** and select the languages for which you want updates.

   - Click **Next.**

3. Select the products for which you want to receive updates.

   - The **Choose Products** page lets you specify the products for which you want updates. Select product categories, such as Windows, or specific products, such as Windows Server 2008. Selecting a product category will cause all the products in that category to be selected.

   - Click **Next.**

4. Choose the classifications of updates.

   - The **Choose Classifications** page allows you to specify the update classifications you want to obtain. Choose all the classifications or a subset of them.

   - Click **Next.**

5. Specify the synchronization schedule for this server.

   - On the **Set Sync Schedule** page, you choose whether to perform synchronization manually or automatically. If you choose **Synchronize manually,** you must start the synchronization process from the WSUS Administration Console. If you choose **Synchronize automatically,** the WSUS server will synchronize at set intervals. Set the time of the **First synchronization** and specify the number of **Synchronizations per day** that you want this server to perform. For example, if you specify that there should be four synchronizations per day, starting at 3:00 a.m., synchronizations will occur at 3:00 a.m., 9:00 a.m., 3:00 p.m., and 9:00 p.m.

   - Click **Next.**

   - On the **Finished** page, you can start the WSUS Administration Console by leaving the **Launch the Windows Server Update Services Administrations snap-in** check box selected, and you can start the first synchronization by leaving the **Begin initial synchronization** check box selected.

   - Click **Finish.**

Step 5: Configure Client Updates This step contains the following procedures:

1. Configure Automatic Updates in Group Policy.

   - In the Group Policy Management Console (GPMC), browse to the GPO on which you want to configure WSUS, and then click **Edit.**

   - In the GPMC, expand **Computer Configuration,** expand **Administrative Templates,** expand **Windows Components,** and then click **Windows Update.**

   - In the details pane, double-click **Configure Automatic Updates.**

   - Click **Enabled,** and then click one of the following options:

     Notify for download and notify for install: This option notifies a logged-on administrative user before the download and before you install the updates.

     Auto download and notify for install: This option automatically begins downloading updates and then notifies a logged-on administrative user before installing the updates.

     Auto download and schedule the install: This option automatically begins downloading updates and then installs the updates on the day and time that you specify.

     Allow local admin to choose setting: This option lets local administrators use Automatic Updates in Control Panel to select a configuration option. For example, they can choose their own scheduled installation time. Local administrators cannot disable Automatic Updates.

   - Click **OK.**

2. Point a client computer to the WSUS server.

   - In the Windows Update details pane, double-click **Specify intranet Microsoft update service location**.

   - Click **Enabled**, and type the HTTP URL of the same WSUS server in the **Set the intranet update service for detecting updates** box and in the **Set the intranet statistics server** box. For example, type *http://servername* in both boxes, and then click **OK**.

3. Manually start detection by the WSUS server.

   - On the client computer, click **Start**, and then click **Run**.

   - Type **cmd** in the **Open** box, and then click **OK**.

   - At the command prompt, type **wuauclt.exe /detectnow**. This command-line option instructs Automatic Updates to contact the WSUS server immediately.

Step 6: Configure Computer Groups This step contains the following procedures:

1. Create a test computer group.

   - In the **WSUS Administration Console**, expand **Computers** and select **All Computers**.

   - Right-click **All Computers** and click **Add Computer Group**.

   - In the **Add Computer Group** dialog box, specify the name of the new test group and click **Add**.

2. Move at least one computer into the test group.

   - In the **WSUS Administration Console**, click **Computers**.

   - Click the group of the computer that you want to assign to the test group.

   - In the list of computers, select the computer or computers that you want to assign to the test group.

   - Right-click **Change Membership**.

   - In the **Set Computer Group Membership** dialog box, select the test group that you created previously, and then click **OK**.

Step 7: Approve and Deploy WSUS Updates This step contains the following procedures:

1. Approve and deploy an update.

   - On the **WSUS Administration Console**, click **Updates**. An update status summary is displayed for **All Updates, Critical Updates, Security Updates,** and **WSUS Updates**.

   - In the All Updates section, click **Updates needed by computers**.

   - On the list of updates, select the updates that you want to approve for installation on your test computer group. Information about a selected update is available in the bottom pane of the **Updates** panel. To select multiple contiguous updates, hold down the Shift key while clicking updates; to select multiple noncontiguous updates, hold down the Ctrl key while clicking updates.

   - Right-click the selection and click **Approve**.

   - In the **Approve Updates** dialog box, select your test group, and then click the down arrow.

   - Click Approved for Install and then click OK.

   - The **Approval Progress** window appears, which shows the progress of the tasks that affect update approval. When approval is completed, click **Close**.

2. Check the status of an update.

   - In the navigation pane of the **WSUS Administration Console**, click **Reports**.

   - On the **Reports** page, click the **Update Status Summary** report. The Updates Report window appears.

   - If you want to filter the list of updates, select the criteria that you want to use, for example, **Include updates in these classifications**, and then click **Run Report** on the window's toolbar.

   - You will see the **Updates Report** pane. You can check the status of individual updates by selecting the update in the left section of the pane. The last section of the report pane shows the status summary of the update.

   - You can save or print this report by clicking the applicable icon on the toolbar. After you test the updates, you can approve the updates for installation on the applicable computer groups in your organization.

Systems Management Server (SMS)

Microsoft offers Systems Management Server (SMS) 2003, which provides more advanced features of administrator management than does WSUS. It gives administrators control over installation and rebooting, helps with compliance reporting, and has a customizable interface.

One of the drawbacks of SMS is that it has frequent updates, which leads to a tedious process of approving, configuring, and deploying. The deployment is very time consuming.

The roles of SMS in the patch management process include the following:

- Installing
- Testing
- Configuring
- Authorizing and distributing
- Rolling back

WSUS Versus SMS 2003

WSUS

- Easy deployment and management of Microsoft updates to servers and clients
- Simple installation and flexible scheduling
- Simple status reporting
- Free service

SMS 2003

- Frequent, time-consuming deployments
- Complex installation and scheduling
- Complex status reporting
- Paid service

Microsoft System Center Configuration Manager 2007

While the Systems Management Server (SMS) eases managing desktop and laptop computers in an enterprise network environment, Configuration Manager builds on the core functionality of SMS, WSUS, Windows Server Active Directory, and the Windows architecture. It provides all the functionality found in Systems Management Server 2003 SP 3 and significantly extends manageability in several key areas.

It is used to enhance the availability, security, and usability of an organization's dynamic IT infrastructure. It comprehensively assesses, deploys, and updates servers, client computers, and devices across physical, virtual, distributed, and mobile environments.

System Center Configuration Manager 2007 includes the following:

- Comprehensive deploying and updating
- Enhanced IT infrastructure insight and control
- Optimization for Windows

Through streamlined, policy-based automation, administrators can centrally manage the full systems life cycle including software update distribution of servers, clients, and mobile devices across physical, virtual, and distributed systems.

Configuration Manager 2007 allows administrators to perform tasks such as:

- Deploying operating systems
- Deploying software applications
- Deploying software updates
- Metering software usage

- Assessing variation from desired configurations
- Taking hardware and software inventory
- Remotely administering computers

Planning and Deploying the Server Infrastructure for System Center Configuration Manager 2007

System Center Configuration Manager 2007 supports many deployment configurations. Administrators need to choose the proper configuration plan for their organization that meets their business requirements. The following are some of the different deployment configurations that Configuration Manager 2007 supports:

- Single-site planning and deployment
- Multiple-site planning and deployment
- Manager sites configuration for optimizing performance
- Upgrade and interoperability planning and deployment
- Manager sites deployment to support Internet-based clients
- Manager sites deployment in international and multilanguage environments
- Manager tasks for decommissioning sites and hierarchies

Planning and Deploying Clients

Client deployment in Configuration Manager 2007 provides a set of tools and resources used to successfully deploy the Configuration Manager 2007 client in an organization's network. The following are the steps for deploying clients in Configuration Manager 2007:

1. Selecting methods used to deploy the Configuration Manager 2007 client software
2. Prerequisites
3. Planning
4. Configuration
5. Troubleshooting
6. Maintenance

Selecting Methods Used to Deploy the Configuration Manager 2007 Client Software The following are the methods for deploying Configuration Manager 2007 client software:

- *Client push installation*: This method is used to target the client to assigned resources.
- *Software update point installation*: This method is used to install the Configuration Manager 2007 client using the Configuration Manager 2007 client software update features.
- *Group policy installation*: This method is used to install the client using Windows group policy.
- *Logon script installation*: This method is used to install the client using a logon script.
- *Manual installation*: This method is used to manually install the client software.
- *Upgrade installation*: This method is used to upgrade the clients to a new version.
- *Client imaging*: This method is used to prestage client installation in an operating system image.

Prerequisites Deploying Configuration Manager 2007 in the organizational environment has many external dependencies and dependencies within the product. These dependencies are automatically installed with the client software. The following are the dependencies that are automatically installed during the installation:

- Microsoft Background Intelligent Transfer Service (BITS)
- Microsoft Windows Installer
- Microsoft Windows Update Agent
- Microsoft Core XML Services (MSXML)

- Microsoft WMI Redistributable Components
- Microsoft Remote Differential Compression (RDC)

Administrators must also make sure that all prerequisites are completed for the specific type of client installation selected.

Planning Before deploying Configuration Manager 2007 clients in the organizational network, administrators need to do the following to plan for successful deployment:

- Decide whether to install a server locator point.
- Decide whether to install a fallback status point.
- Decide which client installation method suits the organization's business needs.
- Decide the optimum throttle settings for the fallback status point.
- Decide how to install Internet-based client management software.
- Determine the need for block configuration manager clients.

Configuration Configuring Configuration Manager 2007 client deployment includes the following tasks:

- Creating a fallback status point in Configuration Manager
- Configuring the fallback status point
- Allocating the fallback status point to Configuration Manager client systems
- Configuring the Configuration Manager client push installation account
- Configuring the request ports for the Configuration Manager client
- Configuring the clients using DNS Publishing to find their management point
- Creating a server locator point in Configuration Manager
- Configuring Configuration Manager client installation properties using Windows group policy
- Configuring the Configuration Manager system client agent

Troubleshooting If administrators experience problems in deploying Configuration Manager 2007 client software, they need to check whether it occurs due to the following issues:

- *Security*: Configuration Manager 2007 uses services to communicate between client and server, and server and server. If the Configuration Manager does not have the proper permissions to connect to the client, it fails to connect to the client.
- *Disk space*: Software packages, updates, inventory, and gathered files use significant amounts of disk space. Administrators need to verify that there is sufficient disk space to expand the site database and to store the required data on the site server.
- *Dependent technologies*: Configuration Manager 2007 has many dependencies on technologies. Sometimes, problems arise due to incorrect configuration and missing prerequisite technologies.
- *Network connectivity*: Administrators need to ensure that the client and server systems are properly connected to each other and can perform name resolution.

Maintenance Based on the site configuration in use, the site maintenance tasks and their schedules can vary. After setting up Configuration Manager 2007, administrators should implement a site maintenance and monitoring plan. There are many predefined site database maintenance tasks that administrators can configure to maintain Configuration Manager 2007 sites, such as the following:

- Backup Configuration Manager site server
- Clear the install flag
- Delete aged client access license data
- Delete aged collected files
- Delete aged configuration management data
- Monitor keys

- Reset AMT computer passwords
- Summarize software metering file usage data

To monitor sites, administrators should look for signs that point out problems and require intervention. The following are some examples:

- File backlog on site servers and site systems
- Status messages that show an error or a problem
- Failing intrasite communication
- Error and warning messages in the computer event log

Configuration Manager 2007 uses Volume Shadow Copy Service (VSS) to create a backup snapshot of its site database. These snapshots are used to backup and restore Configuration Manager sites. Backup data include the following information:

- Configuration Manager site database (SQL Server database)
- Configuration Manager installation directory on the site server
- Master site-control file
- SMS and NAL registry keys on the site server

Security TechCenter

The Security TechCenter provides links to technical bulletins, advisories, tools, prescriptive guidance, and community resources designed to help IT professionals keep Microsoft servers, desktops, and applications up to date and secure. The Web site is at *http://technet.microsoft.com/en-us/security/default.aspx*.

Identifying Missing Patches on Windows Desktop Systems

The following are ways to identify missing patches on Windows desktop systems:

- *Microsoft tools*: Administrators can use Microsoft Baseline Security Analyzer (MBSA) to identify missing patches. It also identifies security issues for Microsoft applications such as MS Office and MS SQL Server.
- *Patch management applications*: Administrators can use patch management tools from third-party vendors such as GFI Software and Shavlik Technologies.
- *Vulnerability scanners*: Administrators can use vulnerability scanners such as Nessus to identify missing patches.

Working with Patch Management Tools

Selecting a Tool

Administrators should keep the following in mind when selecting a patch management application:

- Learning curve
- Ease of use
- Platform support
- System targeting
- Comprehensive testing by a patch management vendor
- Product patch support
- Connection sensitivity
- Deployment schedule
- Cost
- Scalability

Learning Curve

This describes the amount of time it takes to learn how to use the application. A purchased product should be implemented in a short span of time. During the testing, research, and evolution of the project, the administrator needs to determine the competence level and amount of time required to implement the product.

Ease of Use

This determines how easy it is to use the patch management system once it is implemented.

Platform Support

Platform support determines which operating systems the patch management system supports. Different companies use different operating systems; some use Windows XP, some use Windows NT, some use Windows Vista, and so on. The patch management application should support environments that use different operating systems, and it should be able to provide patches to each system.

System Targeting

System targeting is another important aspect that needs to be considered during the process of searching for a patch management application. System targeting allows a patch to be deployed for a selected system based on specific criteria. Some patch management applications can deploy to a range of IP addresses, Windows security groups, and even Active Directory (AD) containers. The administrator needs to determine the level of deployment control required and evaluate the patch management applications accordingly.

Connection Sensitivity

A connection-sensitive patch management tool will allow for the reduction of bandwidth utilization for patch distribution. This process automatically determines the speed and type of connection being used. Connection sensitivity provides information to systems to halt the distribution if the connection is very slow, or uses different methods to initiate the transfer of patches in the background.

Deployment Schedule

A good patch management tool will provide a comprehensive scheduling component. This feature will allow the patch to be transferred to workstations during off-hours. It should provide a high level of control over the patch management process.

Cost

Cost is a major factor for a specific patch management application. A product should be evaluated for its cost, including:

- Total cost for implementation
- Cost of deployment
- Cost of continued management
- Return value against the licensing cost
- Downtime cost

Microsoft Baseline Security Analyzer (MBSA)

The Microsoft Baseline Security Analyzer (MBSA) can determine which significant updates are set up on a target computer, as well as which security updates are needed. MBSA allows users to target the current computer, a remote computer, a particular list of computers, a series of IP addresses, or all computers in a chosen domain. The tool will determine a system's revision status based on a downloaded XML catalog file and will generate a report to either output files or the screen.

MBSA catches common security misconfiguration faults on target computers. It notifies only on the present status of the computer and does not provide users with any distribution responsibility. After a computer is assessed, other tools must be used to position the misplaced service packs and updates. Otherwise, the misplaced service packs and updates must be physically downloaded and installed. MBSA version 1.1 scans for the newest service packs and security updates for the following products:

- Microsoft Windows NT 4.0, Windows 2000, and Windows XP
- IIS 4.0 and IIS 5.0
- SQL Server 7 and SQL Server 2000 (including Microsoft Data Engine)
- Internet Explorer 5.01 or later
- Windows Media Player 6.4 or later
- Microsoft Exchange Server 5.5 and Exchange 2000 Server (including Exchange Admin Tools)

MBSA 2.1 builds on earlier versions, with support for Windows Vista and Windows Server 2008. MBSA 2.1 also provides full 64-bit installation, scan tool and vulnerability assessment (VA) checks, improved SQL Server 2005 checks, and support for the latest Windows Update Agent (WUA) and Microsoft Update technologies.

Scanning for Updates in GUI Mode

By default, MBSA operates in a GUI mode and shows the results on the screen. The scan performed by MBSA only analyzes and reports on updates selected as significant security updates by the Windows Update site.

When scanning for security updates, an administrator follows this procedure:

1. Open MBSA.

2. Select whether to scan either a single computer or multiple computers.

3. For scanning only for security updates, enable the **Check For Security Updates** option, and select **Start Scan**. When the scan is complete, an XML file can be viewed for each computer. For each computer, the output will display any missing security updates for Windows, IIS, Windows Media Player, Exchange Server, and SQL Server, along with a security evaluation rating for the target PC.

Security scan reports are saved in the %userprofile%\SecurityScans folder on the PC where MBSA is implemented. The reports are available in XML format and are best viewed in the MBSA interface.

Scanning for Updates from the Command Line

MBSA has a command-line version executable, Mbsacli.exe, which runs scans for security updates. Version 1.1 of the Mbsacli.exe utility can execute the same tests performed by Shavlik's HfNetChk.exe utility.

When **Mbsacli.exe** is called with the **/hf** switch, indicating an HfNetChk.exe-style scan, all security-relevant updates are incorporated in the scan and the resultant reports. The outcomes of the Mbsacli.exe scan are displayed in the command window, as well as in XML files.

When scanning for security updates with the **Mbsacli.exe /hf** command, the parameters shown in Table 4-2 can be used.

Parameter	Description
-h hostname	Scans the computer named by the NetBIOS computer name. If not present, the local host is scanned. Each hostname is separated with a comma.
-fh filename	Scans the computer names mentioned in the named text file. The text file must have one computer name per line, with a maximum of 256 names.
-i xxx.xxx.xxx.xxx	Scans the named IP address. Multiple IP addresses can be named by separating each entry with a comma.
-fip filename	Scans the IP addresses named in the named text file. The text file must contain one IP address per line, with a maximum of 256 IP addresses.
-r xxx.xxx.xxx.xxx–xxx.xxx.xxx.xxx.	Specifies a range of IP addresses to be scanned.
-d domainname	Specifies that all computer accounts in the named domain name are to be scanned.
-b	Scans exclusively for significant updates, rather than for each security update. This parameter generates the same list of necessary updates as the GUI MBSA.
-s 1	Reduces NOTE messages. NOTE messages do not include an installable executable, but present an elaborate procedure that must be performed to avoid the security susceptibility associated with the update.

Table 4-2   These parameters can be used with Mbsacli.exe /hf   *(continues)*

Parameter	Description
-s 2	Reduces WARNING messages. WARNING messages do not suggest solutions to prevent vulnerabilities. They simply state that the usage of the specific service is considered a security weakness.
-nosum	Specifies that the computer should not perform checksum validation for the security update files.
-z	Specifies that the computer should not perform registry checks.
-v	Displays wordy details when a security update is missing. This is useful when NOTE or WARNING messages are received.
-f filename	Describes the name of a file in which to store the outputs.
-u username	Describes the username to use when scanning a local or remote computer or groups of computers.
-p password	Specifies the password to use when scanning a local or remote computer or groups of computers. This switch must be used with the username switch. This password is not transmitted across the network in plaintext. Instead, Mbsacli.exe implements NT LAN Manager (NTLM) authentication.
-x XMLfile	Specifies an XML data source for the scan. If not specified, the most recent version of MSSecure.xml is downloaded from the Microsoft Web site.

Table 4-2   These parameters can be used with Mbsacli.exe /hf (*continued*)

QChain

The QChain tool facilitates the installation of numerous security updates without needing to reboot between installations. This tool assesses the drivers, DLLs, and executable files revised by each security update and guarantees that only the most current versions of the files are kept after reboot.

To use the QChain tool, a batch file must be created for the security update installation. The following is a sample batch file:

```
@echo offsetlocalset

PATHTOFIXES=c:\patches%PATHTOFIXES%\Q123456_w2k_sp2_x86.exe -z -

m%PATHTOFIXES%\Q123321_w2k_sp2_x86.exe -z -

PATHTOFIXES%\Q123789_w2k_sp2_x86.exe -z -m%PATHTOFIXES%\qchain.exe
```

The batch file configures each security update with the -z switch to avoid reboots after each security update installation and makes use of the -m switch to facilitate unattended installs. After all updates are installed, the QChain tool guarantees that only the most recent versions of updated files are supported.

QChain is not needed for deploying security updates to Microsoft Windows XP or Microsoft Windows 2000 computers with Service Pack 3 or later because QChain functionality is incorporated into these versions.

BES Patch Management

BigFix Patch Management, in combination with the BigFix Enterprise Suite (BES) platform, provides patch management solutions for distributed and multiplatform networks. It has the following features:

- Allows users to view the network's patch compliance status and priority setting to determine what actions are to be taken.
- Remediation, monitoring of patch status, and real-time detection.
- Prepacked and pretested security patches facilitate nearly effortless targeting and deployment.
- Policy-defined patch baselines and endpoint devices guarantee that mobile and remote computers maintain compliance in all environments. The guarantee must be provided even when not connected to the enterprise network.
- The rollback facility prevents undesired consequences obtained from a patch.
- Guarantees that authentic patches are being applied, with the help of incorporated public key infrastructure (PKI) security and secure hash validation of patch packages.

- Provides a complete audit trail of patching actions and patching steps implemented on every system.
- Enables continual implementation of patch compliance using policy-based automation.

Shavlik's HFNetCheck Pro

Shavlik's HFNetCheck Pro supports graphical reporting, displaying patch management information in an attractive and clear manner. Its features include:

- Drag-and-drop patch management interface allows the user to scan the required groups, based on criteria such as what, when, and how the patches must be deployed. The parameters necessary must be set before the deployment, which returns an automated validation indicating the successful installation of patches.
- Security Configuration Management saves organizational costs such as administrative time and provides security related to expensive breaches.
- It enables working with a range of patches through such features as criticality, patch grouping, annotation, machine grouping, machine, and deployment templates. It is best suited for working with multiple administrators.
- It enables the automation of products such as Windows NT, Windows XP, Windows Server 2003, Exchange, SQL Server, Outlook, Microsoft Office, Java Virtual Machine, and non-Microsoft products such as WinZip and Apache.

Shavlik's HFNetCheck Pro has the following benefits:

- Scans large networks (100,000+ machines)
- Scans large numbers of machines concurrently
- Scans organizational units selectively by installing patches and scanning
- Categorizes machines by groups, and imports the list of machines to be scanned
- Useful for scanning required systems, and avoids the scanning of unnecessary systems
- Provides automated e-mail scan results in a graphical format to network administrators
- Provides flexible reboot options where the system can be rebooted according to a particular schedule
- Automated deployment of the missing patches after the completion of the scanning process
- Enables scheduled scans so scanning can be done at low-use time periods, such as weekends

PatchLink Update

PatchLink Update is a tool that provides solutions for patch and vulnerability management for medium and large enterprise networks. It allows the user to translate security policies into an automated security mechanism against vulnerabilities that destroy large enterprise networks. It is an Internet-based security patch and vulnerability management tool for all Microsoft, AIX, HP-UX, Solaris, Linux, Novell NetWare, and Mac OS X operating systems.

PatchLink Update's features include:

- Large enterprise support
- Subscription service customization
- Subscription update optimization
- Client-server communications optimization
- Communication via authenticated proxy

Its key benefits include:

- Enhances administration
- Requires limited WAN resources
- Communicates quickly
- High security

- Enhanced asset management
  - Enhanced standard inventory
  - Customizable inventory
- Contains tracking options for data collection and reporting
- Advanced remediation deployment options
- Deployment deadlines
- Improved end-user deployment experience
- Provides multiple end-user deployment scheduling options
- Simplified agent management
- Discovery and agent installation wizard detects all unprotected devices
- Improved Active Directory and eDirectory discovery ensures simplified setup and execution for these and other LDAP directories
- Flexible Agent Management Center (AMC) installation
- Wake-On-LAN for agent install
- Autopopulation into groups
- Enhanced agent detection
- PC list import
- Improved Macintosh agent integrating the Control Panel and PDDM, providing flexible startup options for process ownership, detection through operation, and reinstallation
- Proactive agent discovery and installation for greater productivity
- Improved agent interface offering more specific information
- Comprehensive discovery and installation for smoother node management

ManageEngine Security Manager Plus

Security Manager Plus (Figure 4-2) is a network security scanner that proactively reports on network vulnerabilities and helps to remediate them and ensure compliance. With vulnerability scanning, patch management, and vulnerability reporting capabilities, it protects the network from security threats and malicious attacks. It support Windows and Linux patch management. The following are some of its patch management features:

- Deploys patches according to a preset baseline
- Automatically sequences the deployment of multiple patches
- Deploys service pack to multiple systems

Altiris Patch Management Solution

Altiris Patch Management Solution, whose Web-based console is shown in Figure 4-3, proactively manages patches and software updates by automating the collection, analysis, and delivery of patches across an enterprise. It helps organizations decrease the costs involved in delivering patches throughout the enterprise. It provides improved functionality in the analysis, collection, and distribution of OS and application updates.

GFI LANguard

GFI LANguard (Figure 4-4) gives administrators what they need to effectively deploy and manage patches on all machines across different Microsoft operating systems. It helps to secure networks faster and more effectively. It provides customizable reports of scans performed across the whole network including applications and resources. The following are some of GFI LANguard's features:

- Identifies security vulnerabilities and takes remedial action
- Automatic remediation of unauthorized applications
- Automatic deployment of networkwide patch and service pack management
- Analyzes and filters scan results

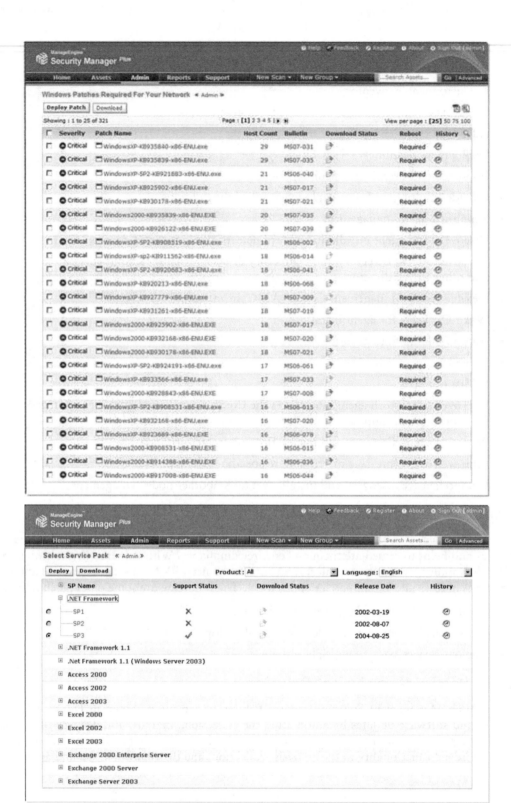

Figure 4-2   Security Manager Plus provides patch management capabilities as part of its network security functionality.

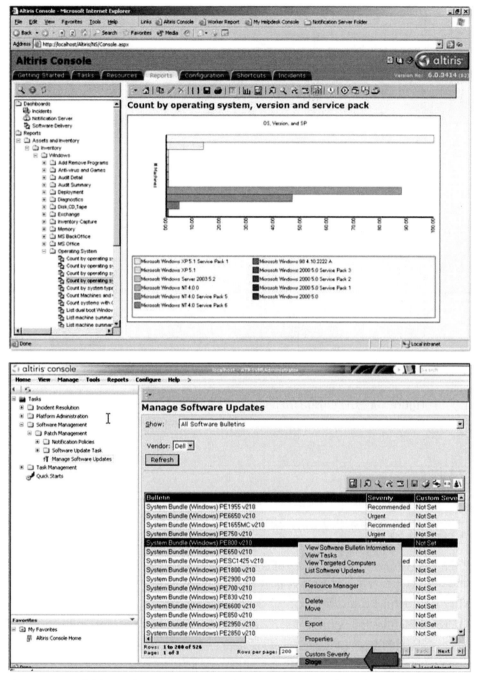

Figure 4-3 Altiris Patch Management Solution automates the collection, analysis, and delivery of patches.

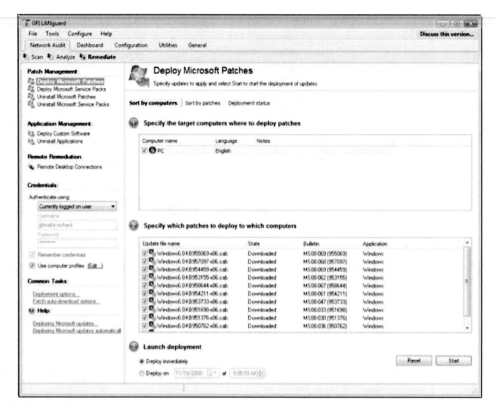

Figure 4-4   GFI LANguard allows administrators to effectively deploy and manage patches across different Microsoft operating systems.

Chapter Summary

- Patch management is the process of controlling the deployment and maintenance of software releases that correct errors in software or provide new features to software.

- Microsoft defines three different types of patches: hotfixes, rollups, and service packs.

- Microsoft defines four different severity ratings: critical, important, moderate, and low.

- Patches should be tested before they are deployed across the enterprise network.

- Red Hat's up2date utility provides patch management services.

- Microsoft Windows Update is a Web-based application that allows users to determine whether new updates are required for a computer.

- Microsoft Software Update Services (SUS) enables the installation of updates from the Internet on desktops and servers.

- Windows Server Update Services (WSUS) is the newer version of Software Update Services (SUS).

- The Microsoft Baseline Security Analyzer (MBSA) can determine which significant updates are set up on a target computer, as well as which security updates are needed.

Review Questions

1. What is patch management?

   _____

   _____

   _____

   _____

2. What are some methods used for updates?

   _____

   _____

   _____

   _____

3. What are the types of Microsoft patches?

   _____

   _____

   _____

   _____

4. What are the severity levels of Microsoft patches?

   _____

   _____

   _____

   _____

5. What is patch testing?

   _____

   _____

   _____

   _____

6. What is a production computer?

   _____

   _____

   _____

   _____

7. What is a test computer?

   _____

   _____

   _____

   _____

8. What is up2date?

_____

_____

_____

_____

9. What are the phases in the patch management process?

_____

_____

_____

_____

10. What is SMS?

_____

_____

_____

_____

11. What is WSUS?

_____

_____

_____

_____

12. What should be considered when selecting a patch management tool?

_____

_____

_____

_____

Hands-On Projects

1. Use Microsoft Baseline Security Analyzer (MBSA) to determine the security state in accordance with Microsoft security recommendations.

   ▪ Navigate to Chapter 4 of the Student Resource Center.

   ▪ Install and launch the Microsoft Baseline Security Analyzer program.

   ▪ Click **Scan Computer.**

   ▪ Type the computer name or IP address.

   ▪ Click **Start Scan.**

   ▪ Click **Results details** to view the results.

   ▪ Click **Scan Multiple Computers** to scan multiple computers.

   ▪ Type the IP address range and click **Start Scan.**

   ▪ Click **View existing security scan reports** to view the reports.

2. Use the MBSA command-line interface tool to scan Windows-based computers for common security misconfigurations and generate individual security reports.

   - Navigate to Chapter 4 of the Student Resource Center.
   - Install and launch the MBSA Command-Line Interface program.
   - Use the tool at the command-line prompt.
   - Use the command **mbsacli /?** to display the user manual.
   - Use the command **mbsacli /target <IP address>** to scan a particular system, where *IP address* is a specific IP address.
   - Use the command **mbsacli /l** to view the list of available scan reports.
   - Use the command **mbsacli /n update** to skip the security update checks while scanning.
   - Use the command **mbsacli /n os** to skip the Windows operating system checks while scanning.
   - Use the command **mbsacli /qp** to skip the scan progress display.
   - Use the command **mbsacli /qr** to skip the scan report list display.
   - Use the command **mbsacli /ls** to display the report of the most recent scan performed.
   - Use the command **mbsacli /xmlout** to display the scan results as XML text.
   - Save the XML report to an output file using the command **mbsacli /xmlout > output.xml**.

3. Read about the economics of security patch management.

   - Navigate to Chapter 4 of the Student Resource Center.
   - Open ECONOMICS OF SECURITY PATCH MANAGEMENT.pdf and read the content.

4. Read about GEO patch management.

   - Navigate to Chapter 4 of the Student Resource Center.
   - Open GEO Patch management.pdf and read the content.

5. Read about patch management.

   - Navigate to Chapter 4 of the Student Resource Center.
   - Open Patch management.pdf and read the content.

6. Read about patch management for EXR Server 3.

   - Navigate to Chapter 4 of the Student Resource Center.
   - Open Patch management for EXR Server3.pdf and read the content.

7. Read about Solaris patch management.

   - Navigate to Chapter 4 of the Student Resource Center.
   - Open Solaris Patch Management.pdf and read the content.

8. Read about creating a patch and vulnerability management program.

   - Navigate to Chapter 4 of the Student Resource Center.
   - Open Creating a Patch and Vulnerability Management Program.pdf and read the content.

9. Read about the total cost of security patch management.

   - Navigate to Chapter 4 of the Student Resource Center.
   - Open The Total Cost of Security Patch Management.pdf and read the content.

Log Analysis

Objectives

After completing this chapter, you should be able to:

- Understand log analysis
- Categorize and analyze Web server log files
- Set up syslog
- Understand monitoring and security events
- Use log analysis and auditing tools
- Use log parsing tools
- Use log file rotation tools
- Understand log security

Key Terms

Active intrusion detection a type of intrusion detection in which security breaches are detected as they happen

Passive intrusion detection a type of intrusion detection that involves reviewing log files to learn about security breaches

Threading how a user navigates through a site

Introduction to Log Analysis

Usually, if something important happens in a computer system, that event is logged somewhere. Log analysis involves investigating firewall, Web server, system, IDS, and Windows event logs to watch for attacks and other important events. This can also help in recovering or restoring lost or corrupted data. This chapter teaches you about several types of logs and how to effectively analyze them.

Audit Policy

Logs usually note any security breaches or malfunctions. Descriptions of notable events are contained in audit logs, including crashes of system programs, system resource exhaustion, and failed login attempts. These types of events are crucial for investigating an attack. Audit data provide important information such as the network address of the system that was used to initiate an attack, the time of the incident, the attack type, whether the attack was a success or failure, and possibly even information about the attacker.

The first target of a skilled attacker will be the audit log system. It is important for the attacker to cover his or her tracks, evading detection as well as keeping the method of attack a secret to prevent the security holes from being fixed.

A security log is maintained to keep a record of valid and invalid login attempts, and events related to creating, opening, or deleting files or other objects. An audit policy defines the types of security events that can be recorded in the security log. This policy helps to minimize the risk of unauthorized access.

Planning an audit policy includes determining what to audit on the computer. In most systems, auditing is turned off by default. After determining what to audit, the audit policies are implemented.

The following are the events that can be audited:

- Account logon events
- Account management
- Directory service access
- Object access
- Policy change
- Privilege use
- Process tracking
- System events

Log Characteristics

There are three characteristics that make each log unique: content, source, and format.

The content of logs is the information contained in them. Alerts, warnings, and fatal errors are combined together into a single "error" log or may be further divided into specific types of errors or sources. In some cases, all log information is combined together into a single file, and its file content helps describe a particular entry.

The log source is used as a method of classification. Logs can come from applications, the system, or drivers and libraries. System logs are generated and handled by the operating system, while application logs are stored either in a central location or in a temporary location.

Logs can be written either in text or binary format. Logs are usually written in plaintext format because it is very easy to work with and can be easily understood by both programs and humans. Binary log information can be formatted by using specific and structured data types. These data types must be known to decipher the data contained in the logs.

Overview of Logging

Logging Requirements

A secure audit log must have tamper resistance, verifiability, data access control, and the ability to be searched.

Tamper Resistance

The creator of the log should be the only one able to create valid entries, and once entries are created, they should be impossible to alter. If any attempts are made to delete the existing entries, they should be detected.

Verifiability

A secure audit log must be verifiable, because it is necessary to regularly check whether entries in the log are present and are not modified.

Audit logs can be either verified publicly or from a trusted verifier. Publicly verifiable audit logs can be verified by anyone who has the appropriate authentication information, such as the logging system's public key or an authenticated hash of all the existing audit entries. Trusted-verifier audit logs can be verified by a designated party holding one or more secrets, such as a MAC key.

The selection of which approach to use is application dependent. Systems that digitally sign the log entries just after they are created make it easy to store the audit logs on untrusted systems. A trusted-verifier system, such as the Schneier and Kelsey scheme, allows a greater degree of forward security.

Data Access Control and Ability to Be Searched

Data in the audit log should be considered sensitive and must be encrypted. Still, it is important for administrators to be able to search the logs. Capabilities must be delegated to allow an investigator to search and view the entries related to an attack. This is a highly sensitive component of the system, so great care must be taken to ensure that only authorized persons can search the logs.

Windows Logging

The Event Log service starts automatically at Windows startup. Application and system logs can be viewed by all users, while security logs can only be accessed by administrators. Security logs are turned off by default, and should be turned on by the administrator.

There are many logs in Windows that can be monitored, including:

- Application logs
- Security logs, which contain a record of logon attempts and the use of resources like creating, opening, and deleting files and objects
- System logs containing system component events like hardware and driver failure issues
- File replication service logs, recording Windows file replication service events
- DNS event logs

Remote Logging in Windows

Log data can be written to a remote share in the network by using the full Universal Naming Convention (UNC) path of the centralized log file store. Before configuring remote logging, Internet Protocol Security (IPSec) should be enabled between the server running IIS and the remote server. If IPSec is not enabled, the log data can be intercepted by malicious individuals and sniffing applications.

As long as the remote computer allows IIS to store the log files on a remote share, IIS creates a log file and writes the data to the remote share. With the help of the following procedure, a remote machine can be configured to allow IIS to create log files on it:

1. On the remote computer, go to the systemroot\System32 folder. Right-click the **LogFiles** folder, and then click **Sharing and Security.**
2. On the **Sharing** tab, click **Share this folder,** and then click **Permissions.**
3. Click **Add.**
4. Click **Object Types.**
5. Check the **Computers** check box, and click **OK.**
6. In the **Enter the object name to select** box, type the object name in the form *Domain\WebServer,* and then click **OK.**
7. In the **Group or user names** list, select the *Domain\WebServer* object, and in the **Permissions** section, check the **Allow** check box next to **Full Control.**
8. In the **Group or user names** list, select **Everyone.**
9. In the **Permissions** section, clear all permissions and click **OK.** The remote computer now has the appropriate access permissions.
10. To set the appropriate file permissions, click the **Security** tab.
11. Select the *Domain\WebServer* object and in the **Permissions** section, check the **Allow** check box next to **Full Control.**
12. Click **Apply,** and then click **OK.**

NTsyslog

This program runs as a service under Windows NT–based operating systems. It formats all system, security, and application events into a single line and sends them to a syslog host.

Its syntax is as follows:

NTsyslog [-install] [-remove]

The -install switch installs the service, while the -remove switch removes it.

The service control manager automatically starts this service during system startup. The service can be started and stopped manually from the Services Control Panel. By default, the service runs under the Local System account. It can be configured to run as a local user with the following rights:

- Log on as a service
- Manage auditing and security log

NTSyslogCtrl is used to configure the types of messages to be monitored and the priority value for each type. The priority for each event log type controls the service and facility that the syslog message is sent to. Each log type has a separate priority. If there is no priority available, it is assigned a priority level of 9.

An entry's priority level is a combination of its facility value and its severity value. To calculate the priority level from normal facility and severity codes, the numeric value for the facility is multiplied by 8, and the numeric value for the severity is added to this.

The standard facility values are:

- (0) kernel
- (1) user
- (2) mail
- (3) system
- (4) security/auth 1
- (5) syslog
- (6) line printer
- (7) news
- (8) uucp
- (9) clock 1
- (10) security/auth 2
- (11) ftp
- (12) ntp
- (13) log audit
- (14) log alert
- (15) clock 2
- (16) local 0
- (17) local 1
- (18) local 2
- (19) local 3
- (20) local 4
- (21) local 5
- (22) local 6
- (23) local 7

The standard severity values are:

- (0) emergency
- (1) alert

- (2) critical
- (3) error
- (4) warning
- (5) notice
- (6) information
- (7) debug

Linux Process Tracking

Process tracking is the audit mechanism for Linux operating systems. It tracks each command that users execute, as well as logon and logoff events. The process tracking file can be found in /var/adm, /var/log, or /usr/adm. This mechanism can be enabled with the accton command. Process accounting logs all messages in its own binary format to /var/log/psacct.

The tracked files can be viewed using the lastcomm command, which will generate output like the following:

```
clear root stdout 0.01 secs Thu Nov 14 07:20
man S root stdout 0.00 secs Thu Nov 14 07:19
sh root stdout 0.01 secs Thu Nov 14 07:19
sh F root stdout 0.00 secs Thu Nov 14 07:19
less root stdout 0.00 secs Thu Nov 14 07:19
crond F root 0.00 secs Thu Nov 14 07:20
mrtg S root 1.02 secs Thu Nov 14 07:20
crond F root ?? 0.00 secs Thu Nov 14 07:20
sadc S root ?? 0.02 secs Thu Nov 14 07:20
```

In this output, the first column shows the processes executed, followed by a flag. The *S* flag stands for the superuser (root), and the *F* flag represents a forked process. Each line also contains the following information:

- How the process was executed
- Who executed the process
- When the process was ended
- Which terminal type was used

Application Logging

The Enterprise Library Logging Application Block simplifies the implementation of common logging functions. Developers can use this logging application block to write information to a variety of locations, including the following:

- The event log
- An e-mail message
- A database
- A message queue
- A text file
- A WMI event
- Custom locations using application block extension points

The logging application block provides a consistent interface to log the information to any destination. Logging behavior can be changed without modifying the application's code.

Firewall Logging

Firewall events fall into three broad categories:

1. Critical system issues
2. Significant authorized administrative events
3. Network connection logs

Generally, the following events are captured:

- Host operating system logs
- Changes to network interfaces
- Changes to firewall policies
- Adding/deleting/changing administrative accounts
- System compromises
- Network connection logs

Reviewing Linux Firewall Logs with grep

The grep command searches one or more files looking for a specific pattern. Its syntax is as follows:

grep [search string][filename]

By default, the search is case sensitive. It can be made case insensitive with the -i switch. The -v switch matches all lines not containing the search string.

To organize the firewall logs, the administrator should first create a file containing all data matching a pattern and then make a second file containing all other data. For instance, to filter for Web server activity from IP address 12.2.21.10, he or she can use the following:

grep '12.2.21.10/80' firewall.log > web-server1.txt
grep -v '12.2.21.10/80' firewall.log > temp-file1.txt

The first command will grab all the traffic going from port 80 on the Web server and record it to the file web-server1.txt. In the second command, all other log entries will be matched and written to the temporary file called temp-file1.txt.

Web Server Logs

Web server log files are text files that usually vary in size from 1 KB to 100 MB. Web servers automatically create and update the following logs:

- access_log
- agent_log
- error_log
- refer_log

In addition, many other pieces of software create their own logs, which will be discussed later in this section.

Access_log

Access_log contains a list of individual files, like HTML and image files, that users have requested from the Web site. Access logs are used to analyze statistics including:

- Total number of visitors to a page
- Origin of users with their domain names
- Total number of requests for each page
- Times the pages were accessed

Below is an example line of text from an access_log:

```
Smx-ca8-50.ix.netcom.com- - [30/Sep/1996:02:57:07 -0400]
"GET /Proj/main.html"
```

Access_log uses three variables for analysis:

1. Domain name
2. Data and time
3. Item accessed

Most Web server log analysis programs mainly concentrate on analyzing access_log. This answers questions such as:

- How many users are accessing the site from a specific top-level domain type (e.g., .com, .edu, .net, .mil, or .gov)? This can also be broken down into domains and subdomains. For example, how many hits has microsoft.com or google.com made to the site? It will also reveal how many hits the server is getting from countries outside the United States.

- How many hits is the server getting during peak hours? These statistics will help network administrators determine the optimal time to perform maintenance and/or upgrades.

- How many hits is every individual page receiving? This statistic can show a webmaster about the most and least successful parts of a site.

The log will also keep statistics about how a user navigates through a site, called *threading*. These statistics include:

- *Entrance*: This indicates what page the user visits first in a session. If a Webmaster puts an announcement only on the home page, users who enter the site through a page other than the home page would not see it.

- *Exit*: This shows what page the user visited before exiting the site. It often shows that a number of users tend to exit the site on a specific page.

- *Clock analysis*: This analyzes the amount of time that a user spends on a specific page. A Web page may have a large number of views, but if the average user is staying on it for a very short amount of time, it may just be used to get to other pages.

- *Download time*: This records the amount of time that users spend to download a page, including graphics. Users access sites with different bandwidth constraints, so a page that takes six seconds to download for one user may take six minutes for another.

Agent_Log

The agent_log records three main things:

1. *Browser*: This indicates the types of browsers used to access the site. There are several Web browsers in use, such as Internet Explorer, Firefox, Safari, and proprietary mobile browsers. Knowing which browsers are used can help Webmasters determine how to design a site.

2. *Version*: This shows the version of the user's Web browser. Users with older versions may not support some features in the Web site design.

3. *Operating system*: To help a Webmaster design a Web site, it is important to know what type of computer and operating system the site's audience is using.

Error_log

The error_log records errors encountered when users browse Web pages. Most errors are usually "File Not Found" errors, but others exist as well. Some errors include:

- *Error 404*: Bookmarks help users to access their favorite pages directly, but URLs change every day. A user who tries to access a Web site using an invalid URL will encounter a 404 error. The error_log tells the Webmaster the time, domain name, and page where this error occurred.

- *Stopped transmission*: When a file download takes too long, the user may cancel the download. Error_log records details of this occurrence, including time, domain name, and referring page. With that information, the Webmaster can redesign the pages to be more efficient.

Most of the time, the percentage of users receiving an error can be greater than 60%. After receiving an error, do users stay or leave? This can be found by using the domain name and time of the user who received an error from the error_log and then looking into the access_log to see whether the domain name shows after the time of the error.

Refer_log

The refer_log indicates which other sites are linking to the local site. For example, if a user on *www.google.com* clicks on a link to *www.sun.com*, then *www.sun.com* will receive an entry in its refer_log. The log will show that the user came to the site via *www.google.com*.

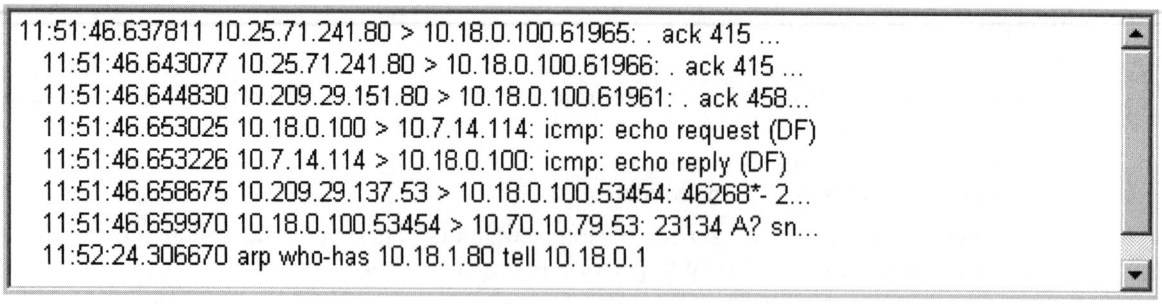

```
11:51:46.637811 10.25.71.241.80 > 10.18.0.100.61965: . ack 415 ...
 11:51:46.643077 10.25.71.241.80 > 10.18.0.100.61966: . ack 415 ...
 11:51:46.644830 10.209.29.151.80 > 10.18.0.100.61961: . ack 458...
 11:51:46.653025 10.18.0.100 > 10.7.14.114: icmp: echo request (DF)
 11:51:46.653226 10.7.14.114 > 10.18.0.100: icmp: echo reply (DF)
 11:51:46.658675 10.209.29.137.53 > 10.18.0.100.53454: 46268*- 2...
 11:51:46.659970 10.18.0.100.53454 > 10.70.10.79.53: 23134 A? sn...
 11:52:24.306670 arp who-has 10.18.1.80 tell 10.18.0.1
```

Figure 5-1   Tcpdump logs contain information about all traffic that passes through the network.

Webmasters should maintain a database of referrals in case URLs change. If a URL changes and the referrers are not notified, users will get 404 errors and simply go somewhere else.

Tcpdump Log

Tcpdump is a program that monitors network traffic. It produces several huge text files, each containing a detailed log of every network packet passed. It allows users to view the entire data portion of an Ethernet frame or other link-layer protocol, and it can print the frame header as well.

Tcpdump gives a clear picture of a specific part of the network, which makes it very useful when something is not working properly. Examining the contents of the traffic can also provide valuable information about the nature of an attack.

Tcpdump can also help restore functionality after denial-of-service attacks. It can provide the source address, destination address, and type of traffic involved if a network is flooded and all other attempts to determine the source and destination of the traffic fail.

Figure 5-1 shows a Tcpdump log.

Apache Logs

Apache Web server logs provide information on user activities and errors. Apache stores nonerror messages and error messages in two separate files. These messages can be split into multiple log files, which is useful when the server has to handle multiple domains.

Default Logs

By default, Apache usually logs general messages to /var/log/httpd/access_log, and it logs error messages to error_log in the same directory. These are usually set by two directives in the httpd.conf configuration file, typically located in the /etc/httpd/conf directory: TransferLog and ErrorLog.

Log Levels

There are several severity levels for error messages for Web server activities. Apache can be set to only record certain levels in order to reduce the sizes of the logs. These log levels, in order from most to least severe, are:

- emerg
- alert
- crit
- error
- warn
- notice
- info
- debug

Log Format

Apache logs are set by the log format directive in the httpd.conf file. The following is a sample entry in the default format:

```
12.127.17.72 - russell [21/Jun/2004:11:50:20 -0500]
"GET /cgi-bin/admin/index.cgi HTTP/1.1" 200 5528
```

Rotating Logs

By default, Apache logs are rotated weekly. Each log file is copied to the next log file, beginning with the next to last and ending with the active log file. If custom logs are created, a log rotation must be set up. This must be done without loss of data while rotating logs and without shutting down Apache for too long. One solution is to write a simple shell script for cron to execute regularly, such as the following:

```
#!/bin/bash
mv -f gen_msg.2 gen_msg.3
mv -f gen_msg.1 gen_msg.2
mv -f gen_msg gen_msg.1
apachectl graceful
```

The first line in the above command tells cron that it is a bash script. The next three lines are used to rename the old log files to their new filenames. The fifth line tells Apache to restart so that the new log file (gen_msg) is created without any current connections getting lost or unrecorded.

IIS Logs

Generally, IIS logs do not capture an intrusion until the request has been processed. However, a diligent administrator might couple logging with tools such as URLScan to catch the attack a little earlier.

IIS log files can be used as clear evidence of an attack. In fact, IIS logs must be treated as evidence by default, in case they are needed for the future prosecution of a hacker. Combining IIS logs with other monitoring records like firewall logs, IDS logs, and Tcpdump can provide more reliability if the log is needed for evidence.

All visits to a Web server are recorded in the IIS log files, which are located at <%systemroot%>\logfiles. If proxies are not used, the IP can be logged.

An administrator should remember these rules when dealing with IIS logs:

- Configure the IIS logs to record each and every available field. Gathering information about Web visitors may establish the source of an attack through a system or a user. The more information collected, the better the chance of tracing the intruder.

- Store events with a proper time stamp. IIS logs use UTC time. Make sure the time zone is set correctly and the system's time is coordinated with NTP.

- Ensure continuity in the logs. An IIS log registers a log entry only if the server gets a hit. This means that an empty log file could mean the server was offline, the log file was deleted, or the server had no hits in that particular day. The easiest workaround is to use the Task Scheduler and schedule hits. These scheduled requests can indicate that the logging mechanism is functioning properly. This means that if a log file is missing, it was intentionally deleted and must be investigated.

- Ensure that logs are not modified in any way after they have been originally recorded. Once a log file is created, it is important to prevent the file from being modified. This can be achieved by moving IIS logs away from the Web server. File signatures are useful to ensure that a single file's corruption will not invalidate the rest of the logs. Also, when doing any log file analysis, copies of the files must be used so that the original files can be preserved in their original state. After a log is closed, no one should have permission to modify its content.

IISLogger

IISLogger produces additional log data and forwards those data to syslog. It even logs data when a Web request is aborted and not completely processed by IIS.

IISLogger is an ISAPI filter, a DLL embedded in the IIS environment. As such, IISLogger starts automatically with IIS. Even if IIS calls an ISAPI filter notification, IISLogger prepares header information and logs this information to syslog.

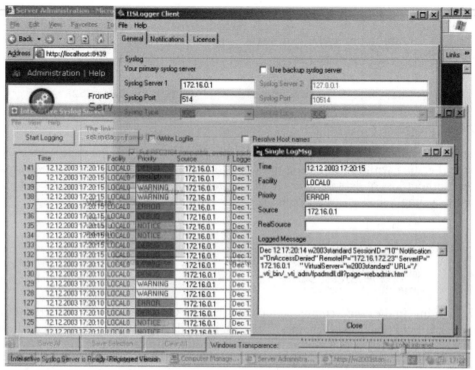

Source: http://www.iislogger.com/en/. Accessed 2004.

Figure 5-2   IISLogger generates additional data and forwards those data to syslog.

IISLogger, shown in Figure 5-2, has the following features:

- Generates additional log information from IIS
- Recognizes hacker attacks
- Forwards IIS log data to syslog
- Is configured using a GUI

Web Server Log Analysis Tools

Analog

Analog analyzes Web server log files and creates HTML, text, or e-mail reports of Web site traffic. Analog is effective for basic reports but does not cover more complex reports such as navigation paths and length of time pages are viewed. Analog can be run from a Web page or from a command line, and can be directly installed on virtual servers. For a smaller site, Analog may be the only program required.

Mach5 FastStats Analyzer

Similar to Analog, FastStats Analyzer generates reports on Web site traffic. It is impressively fast, processing over 200 megabytes per minute. FastStats Analyzer is scalable to any sized Web site and is shown in Figure 5-3.

WebTrends

WebTrends is an easy-to-use Web site traffic tool for Windows. It is commonly used on medium-sized Web sites, meaning sites with more than 150 visitors per day. It provides a full and comprehensive set of reports that can be e-mailed.

Happy Log

Happy Log examines log files and generates reports as lists or graphs. These reports can be viewed as HTML, Word, or Excel files. Figure 5-4 shows one such report.

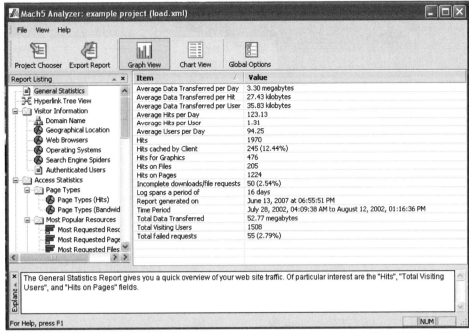

Source: http://www.mach5.com/download/downloadsignup.php?submit1.x=61&submit1.y=24&Name=&Comp.
Accessed 2004.

Figure 5-3   FastStats Analyzer is mainly notable for its speed in analyzing log files.

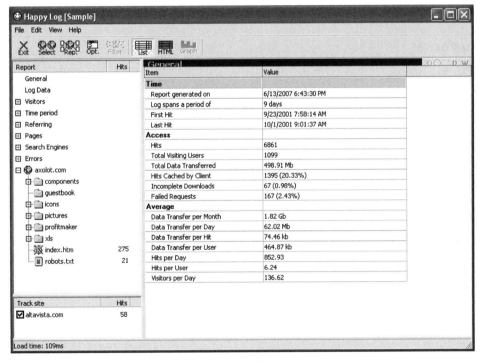

Figure 5-4   Happy Log generates reports as lists or graphs.

Net Merit

Net Merit provides hosted services, giving Web site visitor analytics and monitoring traffic.

ClickTracks

ClickTracks displays visitor behavior directly on the Web site's pages. This makes it easier to understand how visitors are navigating the site. It also generates access_log reports in HTML format.

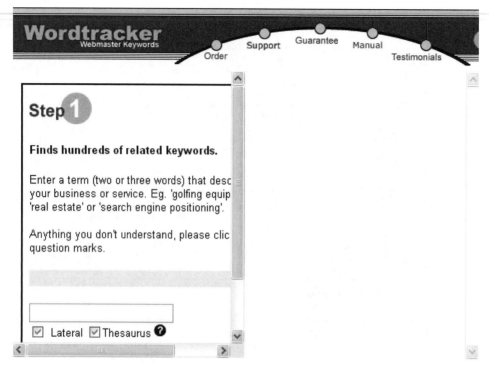

Figure 5-5   Wordtracker will help determine which words are the most useful for improving the site's placement in search results.

Wordtracker

Wordtracker is a tool that determines the current most popular words being used on search engines. This also uncovers which words are unreliable, due to being used by too many other sites. This can help move the site higher in Web search results, driving increased traffic. Wordtracker is shown in Figure 5-5.

Limitations of Log File Analysis

While log file analysis is useful, it does not provide a perfect picture of a site's use. In particular, it has the following limitations:

- In general, log file analysis provides an overestimation of the number of users, because of the difficulty of finding search engines and other bots that index the site.
- Because Web pages are cached on intermediary servers, it is impossible to know the exact number of users accessing the site. Log file analysis only provides the number of users accessing the site directly.
- Most traffic (over 65%) may not be identified by the Internet service provider due to firewalls and other security measures. This makes it difficult or impossible to determine which host is accessing the site.

Syslog

Syslog is a combined audit mechanism used for the Linux operating system and application messages. Syslog supports both local and remote log collection, permitting system administrators to collect and distribute audit data using a single point of management.

Syslog is controlled on a per-machine basis with the file /etc/syslog.conf. The format of configuration lines is:

```
facility.level <Tab> <Tab> action
```

For example, a line in Syslog may be:

```
mail.info <Tab> <Tab> /var/log/maillog
```

Tabs are used to define white space between the selector on the left side of the line and the action on the right side. *Facility* refers to the operating system component or application that generates the log message, and *level* is the severity of the message. *Action* indicates what action is taken based on the facility and level. The system administrator can customize messages based on these factors.

The primary advantage of syslog is that all the reported messages are collected in the message file. To log all messages to a file, the selector and action fields need to be replaced by the wildcard character (*); for example:

```
*.*  /var/log/syslog
```

Logging priorities can be enabled by configuring /var/log/syslog. All messages will be logged with the following priority levels, from most severe to least severe:

- emerg
- alert
- crit
- err
- warning
- notice
- info
- debug

Events such as bad login attempts and the user's last login date are also recorded. If an attacker logs into a Linux server as root using the secure shell service, the attacker's login information will be saved in syslog. Still, the attacker could delete or modify the /var/log/syslog file, erasing evidence of the attack. To avoid this problem, the administrator can set up remote logging.

Building a Central Log Host

By default, syslog messages are stored locally. Automatically routing log files to a centralized location can provide the following benefits:

- Easier to analyze what may have happened
- Difficult for infiltrator to corrupt or alter relocated logs
- Simplifies the archiving of collected logs offline to removable media or even to a printer

A good central log host has a good amount of disk storage and has the single purpose of receiving log messages. A log host should be as secure as possible, with all external services disabled. It should be accessed directly from the console for administration. Normal users should not have accounts on this machine.

Log Parsing

Log parsing is the process of gathering information from a log so that the parsed values can be used as input for another logging process. Parsing is done as part of many other logging functions such as log conversion and log viewing.

Log Normalizing

In log normalization, each log data field is modified so that data are represented similarly between separate log files. The most common use of normalization is storing dates and times in a single format. For example, one log generator might store the event time in a 12-hour format (2:34:56 P.M. EDT) as the *Timestamp* value, while another log generator might store it in 24-hour (14:34) format and call it the *Event Time* value, with the time zone stored in a different notation (−0400) in a different field called *Time Zone*. Normalizing the data makes analysis and reporting much easier when using multiple log formats. However, normalization can be very resource intensive, especially for complex log entries like intrusion detection logs.

Log Storage

System administrators should be able to identify how each log source stores its data. The storage options for log entries are as follows:

- *Not stored*: It may be deemed unnecessary to store some entries that are identified as small or having no value to the organization, such as debugging messages that can only be understood by the software vendor or error messages that do not log any details of the activity.

- *System level only*: These entries might have some value or interest to a system-level administrator, but are not important enough to be sent to the log management infrastructure, and are to be stored on the system. System-level administrators might also find it helpful to review these entries to develop baselines of typical activity and identify long-term trends.

- *Both system level and infrastructure level*: Entries judged to be of particular interest should be saved on the system and also transmitted to the log management infrastructure. Reasons for having the logs in both locations include the following:

  - If either the system or infrastructure logging should fail, the other should still have the log data.

  - During an incident, there is a chance that the attacker will alter the system logs. It is much more difficult for infrastructure logs to be altered. The incident response team can check the infrastructure and system logs to see if there are any differences, which may reveal the data that the attacker attempted to hide.

  - System or security administrators are often responsible for analyzing local logs, but not for analyzing log data on infrastructure log servers. The system logs need to contain all data of interest to the system-level administrators.

- *Infrastructure level only*: If logs are stored on remote servers, it is usually preferable to store at the system level as well. This may not always be possible for systems with low storage capacity or for applications that can only write logs remotely.

Log Rotation

Log sources must be configured to perform log rotation when certain conditions are met, such as at regular time intervals or when a log size exceeds a set limit. If the logging utilities are not capable of rotating logs on their own, administrators must deploy a third-party log rotation tool or utility. If the logger cannot rotate the logs and third-party applications are incompatible, the administrator can choose from the following:

- *Stop logging*: This is an unacceptable option. Logs must always be kept.

- *Overwrite the oldest entries*: This is an acceptable choice for lower-priority log sources, when the significant log entries have already been transmitted to a log server or archived to offline storage. This is a good method for logs that are very difficult to rotate.

- *Stop the log generator*: When logging is critical, it may be necessary to configure the OS, security software, or application generating the logs to shut down when there is no space left for more log entries. In these situations, administrators should take reasonable measures to ensure that log generators have adequate space for their logs and that log usage is monitored closely.

Databases

Databases are used to write severe error and warning conditions to the local syslog. Typically, databases also write errors to a database log file, such as the db2diag.log file on DB2 (one of the first pieces of SQL-based relational database management system software by IBM). These files can be opened in a text editor.

The example following shows a typical entry from the db2diag.log file:

```
Jun 18 15:02:53 bluj DB2[46827]: DB2(db2inst1.000) (1) oper_system_services
sqlobeep(2)
reports: probe id 55 with error 2020 and alert num 0 (3)
Jun 18 15:02:53 (4) bluj (5) DB2[46827(6)]: extra symptom string
provided: RIDS/sqlesysc_ (7)
Jun 18 15:02:53 bluj DB2[46827]: data: 6c65206f 66206c6f 67676564
20646174
Jun 18 15:02:53 bluj DB2[46827]: data: 61
Jun 18 15:02:53 bluj DB2[46827]: data: 54686973 20697320 616e2065
78616d70 (8)
Jun 18 15:02:53 bluj DB2[46827]: 2 piece(s) of dump data provided. . . to
file /u/db2inst1/ (9)
Jun 18 15:02:53 bluj DB2[46827]: 1. 'DUMP EXAMPLE #1' has been dumped (10)
Jun 18 15:02:53 bluj DB2[46827]: 2. 'DUMP EXAMPLE #2' has been dumped
```

The bold numbers in the previous example show the following:

1. The instance name and node number
2. The reporting component and function
3. The probe ID and error and alert numbers
4. A time stamp for when the event occurred
5. The hostname
6. The process ID of the reporting process
7. A symptom string containing additional information about where and why the problem occurred
8. A hexadecimal dump of data that includes return codes and other information for the vendor's support center
9. Information about additional dump files
10. An entry to identify a piece of dump data

Monitoring and Security Events

Monitoring for intrusion and security events includes both active and passive tasks. Many intrusions are identified after the attack has taken place by viewing the log file. Post-attack intrusion detection is known as *passive intrusion detection.* When intrusion attempts are detected during the attack, the administrator is engaging in *active intrusion detection* and can block attack commands as they happen.

Importance of Time Synchronization

Clocks must be synchronized when log data is to be compared between multiple systems. This is the only way an administrator can determine the flow of an attack. If time is not synchronized, it is difficult to identify what events have taken place and how those events are related.

All systems should use the same time source. The Windows 2000 W32Time service provides time synchronization for Windows 2000–based and Windows XP–based computers running in an Active Directory domain. W32Time ensures that the client clocks of Windows 2000–based computers are synchronized with the domain controllers. Kerberos requires this type of synchronization.

Passive Detection Methods

Event logs and application logs are reviewed manually in a passive intrusion detection system. Analysis and detection of attack strategy are done on event log data at the time of inspection. For reviewing the logs, several tools and utilities are available.

EventCombMT

EventCombMT is a multithreaded tool that parses event logs from many servers at the same time, creating a separate thread of execution for each server included in the search criteria. EventCombMT is included with Microsoft Windows Server 2003 Resource Kit Tools and allows the administrator to do the following:

- Define either a single event ID or multiple event IDs to search
- Define a range of event IDs to search; endpoints are inclusive, so to search for all events between and including event ID 528 and event ID 540, the administrator defines the range as $528 < ID < 540$
- Limit the search to specific event logs, including system, application, security, FRS, DNS, and Active Directory logs
- Limit the search to specific event message types, including error, informational, warning, success audit, failure audit, or success events
- Limit the search to specific event sources
- Search for specific text within an event description
- Define specific time intervals to scan back from the current date and time

It is important to note that EventCombMT does not support Boolean operators in search strings, such as AND, OR, and NOT. Also, quotation marks should not be used in search strings.

Scripting

Scripts can be written to collect event log information from remote locations and store it in a central location. These scripts can then be scheduled, and corresponding actions will be taken after the event log is copied to the central location.

The Windows 2000 Resource Kit, Supplement One includes Eventquery.pl. This file is a Perl script that displays events from the Event Viewer logs on local and remote computers running Windows 2000 and offers a wide range of filters to help find specific events.

Log Analysis and Auditing Tools

UserLock

The UserLock tool limits and restricts simultaneous sessions. This provides administrators with remote session control, alert options, and advanced reporting for session analysis. UserLock is shown in Figure 5-6, and its features include the following:

- Simultaneous session prevention and restriction
- Workstation restriction
- Alerts and notifications
- Remote session management
- Connectivity surveillance and monitoring
- Analysis and reporting
- Centralized administration
- Management via Web interface

WSTOOL

WSTOOL is an OS-independent Web vulnerability scanner. It includes:

- SQL injection vulnerability scanning
- XSS (cross-site scripting) vulnerability scanning
- 404/500 server error scanning
- Admin/manage folder search
- Web-based or command-line scanner by PHP

ASDIC

ASDIC (Figure 5-7) is a system for advanced traffic analysis. The features of ASDIC include the following:

- Collects traffic data from various sources like routers, switches, real-time flow monitors, and firewalls
- Converts different kinds of data into a comparable and consistent format
- Stores network sessions in a searchable central database
- Analyzes network flows
- Creates all significant aggregate flows
- Detects anomalies and deviations, and reports events of interest

Tenshi

Tenshi watches multiple log files for the occurrence of a user-defined regular expression. When that expression appears, Tenshi sends e-mail reports detailing where and when it appeared. Regular expressions can also be used for the alert interval and a list of mail recipients. Additionally, uninteresting fields in the log lines (such as PID numbers) can be masked with the standard regular expression grouping operators ( ). This allows for a cleaner and more readable report.

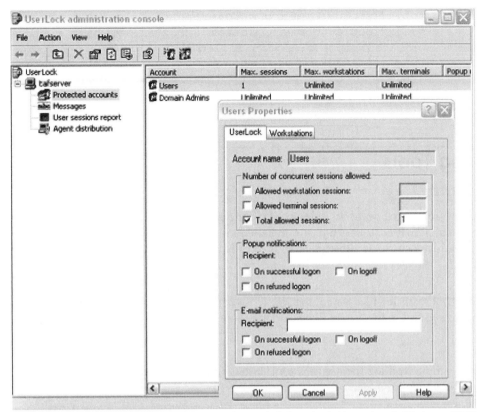

Source: http://www.isdecisions.com/en/software/userlock/screenshots.cfm#20. Accessed 2004.

Figure 5-6   UserLock prevents users from having multiple simultaneous sessions.

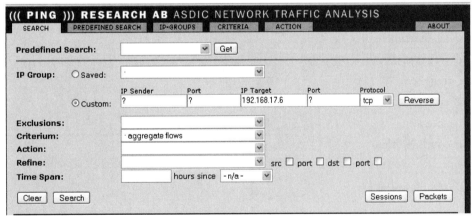

Source: http://info.ping.se/storage/users/3/3/images/23/exempel.png. Accessed 2004.

Figure 5-7   ASDIC helps to determine the types of traffic on the network.

The following is a sample configuration file (tenshi.cnf):

```
. . .
set hidepid on
set queue mail tenshi@localhost sysadmin@localhost [0 */12 * * *]
set queue misc tenshi@localhost sysadmin@localhost [0 */24 * * *]
set queue critical tenshi@localhost sysadmin@localhost [now]
group ^ipop3d:
mail ^ipop3d: Login user=(.+)
mail ^ipop3d: Logout user=(.+)
mail ^ipop3d: pop3s SSL service init from (.+)
mail ^ipop3d: pop3 service init from (.+)
```

```
mail ^ipop3d: Command stream end of file, while reading.+
mail ^ipop3d: Command stream end of file while reading.+
critical ^ipop3d: Login failed.+
trash ^ipop3d:.+
group_end
critical ^sudo: (.+) : TTY=(.+) ; PWD=(.+) ; USER=root ; COMMAND=(.+)
misc .*
```

Log Parsing Tools

LogSentry

LogSentry (formerly Logcheck) is designed to automatically run and check system log files for security violations and unusual activities. It uses a program called logtail that remembers the last position it read in a log file and then uses this position on subsequent runs to only process the new information.

SL2

The SL2 tool scans log files for anomalies. This script reports everything that it finds with the exception of those expressions found in the ignore file, scanlog.ignore.

Flog

Flog is a simple ftpd log file analysis tool. It generates basic statistics about traffic and server utilization, and then outputs them to a file.

Simple Log Clustering Tool (SLCT)

SLCT is a command-line tool designed to find clusters in log files, where each cluster corresponds to a frequently occurring line pattern. Some of the options used with SLCT are:

- -b <byte offset>
- -c <clustertable size>
- -d <regexp>
- -f <regexp>
- -g <slice size>
- -i <seed>
- -o <outliers file>
- -r
- -t <template>

Xlogmaster

Xlogmaster is a program for overall system monitoring. It aids in reading log files, status information, and translations of data. It can apply filters, highlight, and take prescribed actions on user-defined events.

GeekTool

GeekTool for Mac OS is a preference pane to show log files on the desktop background. It can also be used to show the output of shell commands.

Dumpel

Dumpel is a command-line tool that dumps event logs for local or remote systems in a tab-separated text file. It can be used to filter for certain event types. Dumpel's syntax is as follows:

dumpel -f *file* [-s *\\server*] [-l *log* [-m *source*]] [-e *n1 n2 n3*. . .] [-r] [-t] [-d *x*]

Table 5-1 shows the arguments for Dumpel.

Argument	Description
-f *file*	Specifies the filename for the output file. There is no default, so a filename must be specified.
-s *server*	Specifies the server where the event log will be dumped. Leading backslashes on the server name are optional.
-l *log*	Specifies which log (system, application, security) to dump. If an invalid log name is specified, the application log is dumped.
-m *source*	Specifies from which source (such as rdr or serial) to dump records. Only one source can be supplied. If this switch is not used, all the events are dumped. If a source is used that is not registered in the registry, the application log is searched for records of this type.
-e *n1 n2 n3*	Filters for event id *nn* (up to 10 can be specified). If the -r switch is not used, only records of these types are dumped. If -r is used, all records except records of these types are dumped. If this switch is not used, all events from the specified source are selected. This switch cannot be used without the -m switch.
-r	Specifies whether to filter out specific sources or records.
-t	Specifies that individual strings are separated by tabs. If -t is not used, strings are separated by spaces.
-d *x*	Dumps events for the past *x* days.

Table 5-1   These are the arguments that can be used with Dumpel

2/7/2007	12:52:25 PM	4	0	1000	LoadPerf	N/A	USER	Performance counters for the RSVP (QoS RSVP) service were loaded successfully. The Record Data contains the new index values
2/7/2007	12:52:26 PM	4	0	1000	LoadPerf	N/A	USER	Performance counters for the PSched (PSched) service were loaded successfully. The Record Data contains the new index values
2/7/2007	12:52:50 PM	4	0	1000	LoadPerf	N/A	USER	Performance counters for the RemoteAccess (Routing and Remote Access) service were loaded successfully. The Record Data contains the new index values assigned to this service.
2/7/2007	12:56:44 PM	4	0	1000	LoadPerf	N/A	USER	Performance counters for the TermService (Terminal Services) service were loaded successfully. The Record Data contains the
2/7/2007	12:56:47 PM	4	0	1000	LoadPerf	N/A	USER	Performance counters for the MSDTC (MSDTC) service were loaded successfully. The Record Data contains the new index values
2/7/2007	12:56:49 PM	4	1	4104	MSDTC	N/A	USER	
2/7/2007	12:56:50 PM	4	2	2444	MSDTC	N/A	USER	0 0 0 0 0 0
2/7/2007	12:57:12 PM	4	0	1000	LoadPerf	N/A	USER	Performance counters for the WmiApRpl (WmiApRpl) service were loaded successfully. The Record Data contains the new index
2/7/2007	12:57:13 PM	4	0	1001	LoadPerf	N/A	USER	Performance counters for the WmiApRpl (WmiApRpl) service were removed successfully. The Record Data contains the new values of the system Last Counter and Last Help registry entries.
2/7/2007	12:57:13 PM	4	0	1000	LoadPerf	N/A	USER	Performance counters for the WmiApRpl (WmiApRpl) service were loaded successfully. The Record Data contains the new index
2/7/2007	12:57:20 PM	2	0	63	WinMgmt	NT AUTHORIT	USER	
2/7/2007	12:57:22 PM	2	0	63	WinMgmt	NT AUTHORIT	USER	
2/7/2007	12:57:22 PM	2	0	63	WinMgmt	NT AUTHORIT	USER	

Figure 5-8   This is a sample log captured by Dumpel.

For example, to dump the local application log to a file named event1.out and get all events except ones from the garbase source, the user types the following command:

dumpel -f event1.out -l application -m garbase -r

Figure 5-8 shows a sample log captured by Dumpel.

Watchlog

Watchlog is a Perl program designed to give a better real-time view of Web traffic. Watchlog uses a tracing log file to show only relevant data.

LogDog

LogDog monitors the messages that pass through syslogd and triggers an action based on keywords and phrases. The configuration file in LogDog specifies which keywords and phrases should generate alerts. It also specifies

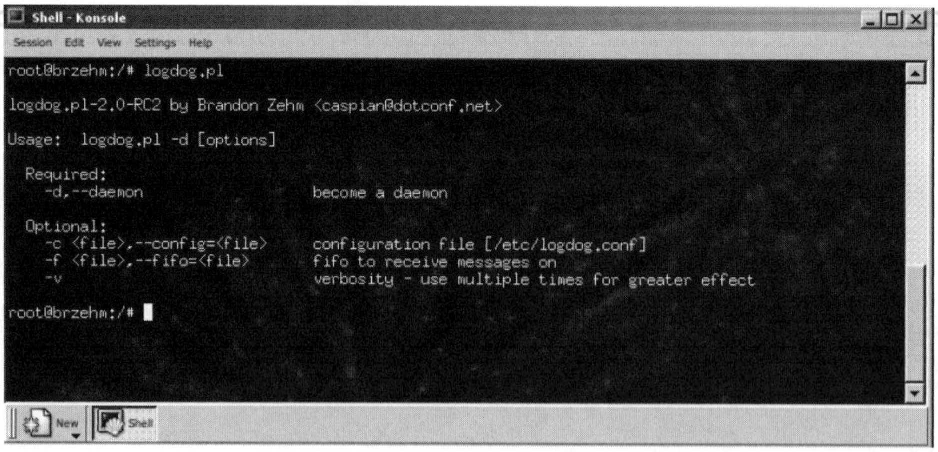

Source: http://caspian.dotconf.net/menu/Software/LogDog/. Accessed 2004.

Figure 5-9   LogDog monitors syslogd and triggers actions when it finds user-specified words and phrases.

a list of commands to be triggered when these words are encountered. LogDog is shown in Figure 5-9, and its features include:

- Monitors syslogd messages for keywords and phrases, and runs system commands based on the content
- Logs all activity to a file
- Reads data from syslogd via FIFO for efficiency and low-latency alerts
- Script returns error status to the system when an error occurs
- Verbose and descriptive error messages
- Multiple debugging levels

Log File Rotation Tools

LogController

LogController restricts the size of log files that become too large. If any log file goes beyond the configured size limit, it is automatically truncated to a new user-defined size. The removed data is then stored in another file.

Newsyslog

Newsyslog is a highly configurable program for managing and archiving log files. It has the following features:

- Portable (using GNU Autoconf) and can be compiled and installed on most modern UNIX or UNIX-like systems
- Supports fixed time-of-day daily archiving with a command-line option to identify the daily rollover time
- Supports the FreeBSD feature that allows specification of the log rollover time as a daily, weekly, or monthly interval
- Supports optional PID files so that nonstandard daemons can be told to reopen their log files after archiving has taken place
- Can leave the most recently archived log file uncompressed, which is necessary for daemons like httpd and smail, because they continue to write to the current log file until their current jobs have been completed
- Supports the FreeBSD feature of being able to restrict processing to just those log files specified on the command line
- Parses the configuration file before taking any action, meaning that if any errors are encountered, it will report them and quit without doing anything
- Rolls a log file if either the interval or size limits have been reached
- Uses an advisory lock on the current configuration file to prevent multiple invocations from tripping over each other

Spinlogs

Spinlogs is a shell script for rotating system logs. It can be configured through a text file and used by UNIX systems running ksh. Many options are available to specify how and when log files are rotated, and the configuration file is very straightforward.

Trimlog

Trimlog is used to trim system log files larger than a specified limit. When invoked, it reads commands from its configuration file that tell it which files to trim, how to trim them, and by how much they should be trimmed.

System Log Rotation Service (SLRS)

The System Log Rotation Service (SLRS) is a tool that automates rotation of collected UNIX system log files. All included systems and their managed log files are centralized, which helps when troubleshooting difficult system or network problems. This utility also provides the following capabilities on a per-log-file basis:

- Unique definable size threshold
- Optional automatic compression of the rotated log file
- Self-purging of the rotated log file when the age of the rotated file exceeds a definable limit
- Daemon notification when the log file is rotated
- Optionally bypass the rotation on defined hosts
- Definable protections and destinations for the rotated log files

Securing Logs

Because they contain sensitive and critical data, it is imperative that administrators protect the integrity, availability, and confidentiality of log data. Security considerations for log files include the following:

- *Limit access to log files*: All users must have some access to log files to be able to create log entries. Most users should have append-only privileges and no read access. Operations such as renaming, deleting, and other file operations on the log files must be reserved to administrators.
- *Avoid recording unneeded sensitive data*: Some logs record sensitive but unnecessary data like passwords. This information should not be recorded because it presents a substantial risk.
- *Protect archived log files*: It is important to secure the message digest for the files, encrypt the log files, and provide adequate physical protection for the archival media.
- *Secure the process that generates log entries*: Access and manipulation of the log source process should not be done by unauthorized parties. Execution of files, configuration of files, and other components of log sources must be protected.
- *Configure each log source to behave appropriately when logging errors occur*: Logging sources should be configured to stop functioning when logging fails.
- *Implement secure mechanisms for transporting log data*: The transportation of log data from various systems to the centralized log management server is important, but transport protocols like HTTP and FTP cannot provide adequate protection. Logging software should always be kept up to date to ensure that the latest security features are used. Logging communication should be done through IPSec or SSL.

Chapter Summary

- Audit logs contain descriptions of notable events, including crashes of system programs, system resource exhaustion, and failed login attempts.
- There are three characteristics that make each log unique: content, source, and format.
- A secure audit log must have tamper resistance, verifiability, data access control, and the ability to be searched.

- Web servers automatically create and update the following logs: access_log, agent_log, error_log, and refer_log.
- Apache Web server logs provide information on user activities and errors.
- Syslog is a combined audit mechanism used for the Linux operating system and application messages.
- Log sources must be configured to perform log rotation when certain conditions are met, such as at regular time intervals or when a log size exceeds a set limit.

Review Questions

1. What is log analysis?

   _____

   _____

   _____

   _____

2. What events can be audited?

   _____

   _____

   _____

   _____

3. What are the components of a log?

   _____

   _____

   _____

   _____

4. What are the four main types of Web server logs?

   _____

   _____

   _____

   _____

5. What are some tools for analyzing Web server logs?

   _____

   _____

   _____

   _____

6. What is log parsing?

   _____

   _____

   _____

   _____

7. What is log rotation?

_____

_____

_____

_____

8. What are the different types of Windows logs?

_____

_____

_____

_____

9. When keeping and analyzing logs, why is it important that time be synchronized in computer systems?

_____

_____

_____

_____

10. What is Dumpel?

_____

_____

_____

_____

11. What are some important steps to ensure log security?

_____

_____

_____

_____

Hands-On Projects

1. Use Kiwi Syslog Daemon to receive, log, display, and forward syslog messages and SNMP traps.

   ▪ Navigate to Chapter 5 of the Student Resource Center.

   ▪ Install and launch the Kiwi Syslog Daemon program.

   ▪ Click **New** in the **Kiwi Service Manager** window to create a new rule.

   ▪ Click **Rules** in the **Kiwi Syslog Daemon Setup** window.

   ▪ Click **Add rule** to create a new rule.

   ▪ Type the name of the rule or rename it.

   ▪ Click **Create New Item**.

   ▪ Name the new filter.

   ▪ From the **Field** drop-down menu, select **IP address**.

   ▪ From the **Filter Type** drop-down menu, select **Simple**.

- Enter the IP address from which messages should be ignored in the **Include** text box.
- Click **Add filter**.
- From the **Field** and **Filter Type** drop-down menus, select the filter name and filter type.
- In the **Include** text box, type "PPP Connected" "PPP Disconnected". The search items must be in double quotes ("").
- To test the filter, click **Test**.
- Right-click **Action** and select **Add action** to create an action.
- Select the action from the drop-down menu.
- Click **Apply**.
- Click **File** and select **Send text message to localhost**.

2. Use the Dumpel event log command-line tool to dump an event log for a local system or a remote system into a tab-separated text file.

   - Navigate to Chapter 5 of the Student Resource Center.
   - Run the Dumpel tool from the command prompt and try some of its options. Its syntax is:

     dumpel –f file[-s\\server][-l log[-m source]][-e n1 n2 n3. . .][-r][-t][-d x]

   - To dump the local system event log to a file named event.out and only get rdr events 2013, use:

     dumpel -f event.out -l system -m rdr -e 2013

   - To dump the local application log to a file named event.out and get all events except ones from the garbase source, use:

     dumpel -f event.out -l application -m garbase -r

3. Read an introduction to log analysis.

   - Navigate to Chapter 5 of the Student Resource Center.
   - Open Introduction to Log Analysis.pdf and read the content.

4. Read the top five log analysis mistakes.

   - Navigate to Chapter 5 of the Student Resource Center.
   - Open Top 5 Log Analysis Mistakes.pdf and read the content.

5. Read about monitoring IIS logs.

   - Navigate to Chapter 5 of the Student Resource Center.
   - Open Monitoring-IIS-Logs.pdf and read the content.

6. Read how to build an encrypted and searchable audit log.

   - Navigate to Chapter 5 of the Student Resource Center.
   - Open Building an Encrypted and Searchable Audit Log.pdf and read the content.

7. Read about detecting intrusions with a firewall log.

   - Navigate to Chapter 5 of the Student Resource Center.
   - Open Detecting Intrusions with your Firewall Log and OsHids.pdf and read the content.

Chapter 6

Application Security

Objectives

After completing this chapter, you should be able to:

- Identify the difficulties in Web security
- Identify application threats and their countermeasures
- Secure Web applications
- Utilize embedded application security
- Implement remote administration security
- Understand threat modeling

Key Terms

Interfaces   external gateways to applications

Introduction to Application Security

A variety of software is now being used in online transactions. Web-based applications are readily available throughout the world, which means their security can be challenged at any time. Therefore, proper measures must be taken to minimize risks and secure applications with the newest available technology. This chapter teaches you about various forms of application security and how to implement them.

Difficulties in Web Security

The main problems with Web security involve managing Web browser activity. It is difficult to identify errors on a Web page when dealing with tags and identifiers. The Web includes the following components:

- Servers (IIS, Apache, etc.)
- Applications (written in Perl, PHP, Python, Java, JavaScript, C, Tcl, etc.)

- Browsers (Mozilla, Internet Explorer, Safari, Lynx, Opera, and mobile browsers) and custom scripts
- Diverse technologies (HTTP, HTML, XML, SSL, SQL, RSS, encryption, cookies, and Webcasts)
- Operating systems (Linux, UNIX, Windows, and Mac OS)

Effective Web security means that all combinations of the above must be considered and secured.

Application Threats and Countermeasures

A threat is the occurrence of any event or circumstance that could harm assets. Application threats can be categorized further.

Input Validation

This includes any kind of input provided by a user that will make an application perform in a way the developers did not intend. It can involve the type, range, or format of input data. To minimize input validation threats, developers must follow these guidelines:

- Do not trust that input will be valid. Provided input could be malicious, so it needs to be verified. Centralized input validation ensures validation rules are followed.
- Never trust client-side validation.
- Check whether the input data are correct. If the input data are correct, allow the data to flow, but if the data are malicious, discard it or make it valid input.

Buffer Overflow

Buffer overflow threats include denial-of-service (DoS) attacks and code injection attacks that cause legitimate users to be denied the use of specific resources. These can be avoided by using the following countermeasures:

- Checking the input's type and length, to catch unexpected input
- Limiting unmanaged code for the application
- Auditing the managed code

Cross-Site Scripting

Cross-site scripting causes different code to be executed from another site. To prevent this, developers should implement input validation checks on query strings and form fields. They should check to be sure cookies are valid, and they should make use of the functions HTMLEncode and URLEncode to encode any output.

SQL Injection

SQL injection attacks inject malicious commands into SQL database queries. The main countermeasures for this include:

- Applying input checks before sending requests to the database
- Applying parameterized stored procedures
- Not allowing restricted users to connect to the database

Canonicalization

Canonicalization is the process of transforming a flexible data structure into one that has specifically defined characteristics. It is a technique for validating input data. When canonicalization is required, the administrator can use the following to ensure that the input only occurs once:

- Using absolute file paths instead of relative paths
- Ensuring that filenames are standard and relevant to the application
- Ensuring that proper character encoding is used

Authentication

Authentication ensures that only legitimate users can access applications. Administrators should keep the following guidelines in mind to defend against authentication attacks:

- Public and confidential information should be kept as separate as possible.
- Support password expiration. The longer a password is kept in use, the less secure it becomes.
- When the system is attacked, disabling accounts used during the attack helps prevent further attacks.
- Never save passwords in user accounts. When a user account is attacked, the attacker's job becomes significantly easier if the password is saved.
- Create strong passwords. Try to create them with a mixture of uppercase and lowercase letters, numbers, and special characters.
- Never send passwords in plaintext. Information sent across the network in plaintext form can be easily accessed.
- Protect authentication cookies. Cookies should have expiration dates built into them.

Network Eavesdropping

In network eavesdropping, the attacker intercepts a username and password from the network when a user sends them to the server. The best way to prevent network eavesdropping is to use authentication mechanisms such as Kerberos or Microsoft Windows authentication along with encrypted passwords.

Brute-Force Attacks

Brute-force attacks simply involve trying as many combinations of characters as possible to try to guess a password. Using strong passwords minimizes the risk of brute-force attacks.

Dictionary Attacks

This technique is like a brute-force attack, except it simply goes through words in the dictionary and tries each of them as the password until one works. This attack can be avoided by using complex passwords made of uppercase, lowercase, numeric, and special characters. The risk due to dictionary attacks can be completely eliminated by using cryptographically strong random numbers in the password.

Cookie Replay Attacks

Cookie replay attacks involve capturing cookies to gain access under a false identity. Countermeasures to prevent cookie replay attacks include applying an encrypted communication channel and applying a timeout for cookies.

Credential Theft

Credential theft is stealing someone's login and password after it has been saved on the system. Countermeasures to help prevent credential theft include:

- Applying strong passwords
- Storing password verifiers in hash form
- Using an account lockout policy after a specific number of retry attempts

Authorization

Authorization allows users to access a specific resource or service. Administrators should be sure to allow users to only use the resources that they need and place a security checkpoint before users are allowed to perform any sensitive application-related function. Administrators should use IPSec on the server when communicating with other servers.

Elevation of Privileges

Elevation of privileges involves an attacker gaining the privileges of the local administrator to have full control over the machine or system. The primary countermeasure to avoid elevation of privileges is to use the principle of least-privileged processes, services, and user accounts. This restricts the lower-level user accounts to only those processes that are absolutely necessary to perform the assigned operation, and make it much more difficult for an attacker who gains access to the low-level account to avoid those access controls and escalate privileged access.

Disclosure of Confidential Data

Confidential data, including application-specific data, must be protected from unauthorized users. This data must be kept in persistent stores like databases and configuration files. Countermeasures to prevent the disclosure of confidential data include:

- Creating roles for specific users to access confidential data
- Making strong access control lists (ACLs) to secure Windows resources
- Using standard encryption to keep confidential data in configuration files and databases

Data Tampering

Data tampering involves the unauthorized modification of data. The main countermeasures in preventing data tampering are creating roles for specific users to access confidential data and allowing data to be modified only by authorized users.

Luring Attacks

This is an attack in which a lower-privileged user tricks a higher-privileged component into running a process that performs malicious activities. The main countermeasure to avoid luring attacks is to restrict access to trusted code to users with proper authorization.

Configuration Management

Configuration management permits operators and administrators to alter configuration parameters, update Web site content, and perform routine maintenance. Attackers and intruders can probe configuration management functions that can potentially damage the Web site, disable the application, or corrupt configuration data. The main countermeasures include:

- Providing only a few administration interfaces
- Having strong authentication
- Using strong authorization with multiple gatekeepers
- Using secured channels for remote administration
- Giving users the least privileges necessary

Unauthorized Access to Configuration Stores   Configuration stores keep confidential data and must be properly secured. These stores should be secured by using restricted ACLs on text-based configuration files, such as Machine.config and Web.config, and custom configuration stores outside the Web space so that Web server configurations are not visible to outside users.

Retrieval of Plaintext Configuration Secrets   Configuration stores must be kept encrypted through passwords and connection strings. This helps in keeping external attackers, as well as lower-level users, from gaining sensitive configuration data and account credentials.

Lack of Individual Accountability

There must be proper auditing tools to keep track of users logging in and out. Any malicious changes made by users must be corrected immediately. This includes all accounts, administrative and otherwise.

Overprivileged Application and Service Accounts

An attacker can manipulate excess privileges given to user accounts. Therefore, it is suggested to give accounts the least privileges necessary.

Sensitive Data

Sensitive data are the most critical data that intruders could steal or modify. Measures to protect sensitive data include:

- Using restricted ACLs on persistent data stores
- Storing encrypted data
- Using identity and role-based authorization
- Using encrypted communication channels like Secure Sockets Layer (SSL)
- Using tamper-resistant protocols like Hashed Message Authentication Codes (HMACs)
- Never storing passwords in plaintext on the system

Session Management

Session hijacking is a serious threat in which the attacker captures the authentication token representing a user's session. Other threats include session replay, in which the user's session token is captured and presented by an attacker to avoid the authentication mechanism, and man-in-the-middle attacks, when the attacker intercepts messages between the sender and recipient.

Countermeasures to prevent session threats include:

- Using an encrypted communication channel such as SSL and using HTTPS connections to float cookies: When an application is accessed via the rewrite engine, as is the case with encrypted communications, the cookies will not be stored on the user's browser. They will be stored on the security authority itself and will be transparent to any client-side code that relies on cookies. This is known as *floating the cookies.*
- Requiring that every session has login functionality for authentic use
- Applying an expiration time to cookies and session tokens
- Applying reauthentication when performing critical operations
- Making a "do not remember me" option to prevent users from storing session data
- Using encrypted data during transmissions
- Using HMACs
- Always encrypting authentication cookies

Cryptography

Cryptography refers to the encryption of data. The main problems involved in cryptography are poor key generation/management, weak encryption, and checksum spoofing. Cryptography includes:

- Applying strong built-in encryption routines involved in secure key management
- Applying strong random-key generation functions
- Storing the key in a restricted location
- Encrypting the encryption key using the Data Protection Application Programming Interface (DPAPI)
- Setting keys to expire at regular intervals
- Developing strong customized algorithms
- Applying proven cryptographic services on a particular platform
- Avoiding cracked algorithms and understanding the techniques used to crack them

Parameter Manipulation

In this technique, a parameter is modified between the client and Web application functions. This can include query string manipulation by HTTP GET from the client to the server, form field manipulation by client-side validation routines bypassed from the HTTP POST protocol, cookie manipulation, and HTTP header manipulation. To counter this threat, administrators should consider the following measures:

- Identifying the client using a session identifier instead of keeping sensitive or critical data in the parameters
- Using HTTP POST instead of GET to submit forms

- Encrypting query string parameters
- Using encrypted communication channels like SSL
- Using HTTPS connections to float cookies
- Encrypting cookie parameters
- Never making security decisions based on HTTP headers

Exception Management

Exceptions reveal useful information to attackers. Applications that do not use exception handling or implement it poorly may suffer from denial-of-service (DoS) attacks. The main countermeasures include:

- Applying exception handling throughout the application's code base
- Handling and logging exceptions at the application boundary
- Providing generic and harmless error messages to the user
- Providing input validation checks

Auditing and Logging

Auditing and logging help to trace suspicious activities such as footprinting or password-cracking attempts. Attackers will usually try to cover their tracks, but some trace may still exist. Administrators should consider these steps to find remnants of an attack:

1. Audit and log activity on the Web server, database server, and application server.
2. Secure and maintain backups of log files.
3. Log key events such as transactions and login and logout events.
4. Never use shared accounts, because the original source of an action cannot be traced when accounts are shared.
5. Log critical application-level operations.
6. Use platform-level auditing to:
   - Audit login and logout events
   - Access file systems
   - Investigate failed object-access attempts
   - Continuously get backup log files and analyze them for signs of suspicious activity
   - Secure log files by using restricted ACLs
   - Relocate system log files

Securing Web Applications

When using Web applications, security is extremely important, because data regularly flow in and out of the network, and these data must be protected.

Managing Sessions

A server creates a temporary session to recognize a user when the user makes a page request. That way, when the same user goes to another page on the site, the server can identify that user. The temporary session can be used to track user activity and allow users to customize the way pages are displayed.

An API is provided by the application server and uses session management to identify the users across multiple page requests. For session management, every server has its own set of APIs.

Managing Sessions in Active Server Pages (ASP)

When using an Active Server Pages (ASP) session object, the server creates an object and special user ID. Applications can then be created to recognize each visiting user, gather information, and then use that information to track user preferences or selections.

The user ID created by ASP is the same as a cookie. Due to this, if users create applications for browsers that do not support cookies, or if customers set their browsers to reject cookies, then ASP's session management features cannot be used.

Cookies

Because HTTP is a stateless protocol, after each request, the server forgets every request made before it. This makes it difficult to maintain sessions, so the server might send a cookie to the user. A cookie is a small text file stored on the user's hard disk, containing information such as user ID, preferences, shopping cart information, and other Personally Identifiable Information (PII).

Cookies can be created in Perl, JavaScript, ASP, and others. If the user already has a cookie on the system, the browser transfers that cookie to the site at every visit. The domain name of the site and path of the application are part of the cookie. The cookie will not be transferred unless the domain name and path match exactly as they were set. There is no way to see the content of one site's cookie on another site.

Persistent Versus Nonpersistent Cookies

A persistent cookie is stored on the client and is valid until it expires or until the user deletes it. Persistent cookies are used to collect user information such as Web surfing behavior or preferences for a particular site. Nonpersistent cookies are stored in the client's RAM and expire when the browser is closed or when the cookie is explicitly destroyed by a logoff script.

Secure Versus Nonsecure Cookies

Secure cookies can only be transferred over HTTPS, while nonsecure cookies can be transferred over HTTPS or regular HTTP. A secure cookie provides only transport security. Once the client receives the data, the end user is in complete control of the data, regardless of the transport mechanism in use.

Session Tokens

Every session token must be unique, nonpredictable, and resistant to reverse engineering. The token must be generated using a reliable random number, obtained from a source like a pseudorandom number generator, Yarrow, or EGADS. Session tokens should be attached to a particular HTTP client instance to avoid hijacking and repeated attacks. In general, a session-token algorithm should not be based on the use of variables, especially user information.

Even if cryptographically strong algorithms are used, attackers can use automated brute-force scripts if the key space is not large enough.

Authentication tokens are security devices provided to authorize users who maintain the tokens in their custody. The security token can be read in the same way as a credit card, or it can include a constantly changing number as a password. These can be implemented entirely in software, or hardware authentication tokens can be used that can plug directly into a computer's USB port.

Encrypting Private Data

Encryption is a method of converting information into a secret form, so that it is understandable only by those who know how to decrypt it to recover the original message. This is especially important for data transmitted via an unsecured network like the Internet.

There are encryption tools available to secure the following:

- Stored data in a single file or in an entire network
- Computer code, such as an operating system
- Information on the Internet, such as e-mails and Internet telephony
- Communication infrastructures, such as wireless networks

Note Studio

Note Studio provides real encryption for private data. Unlike encryption algorithms, it actually changes the contents of a file so it can no longer be found on the file system. Note Studio uses a three-way encryption method for increased security and can be seen in Figure 6-1.

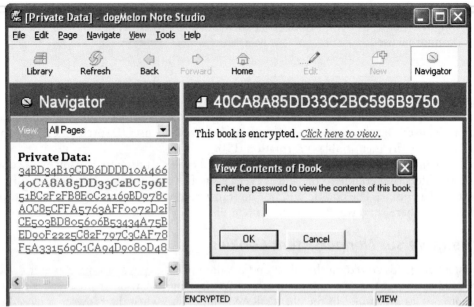

Source: http://www.dogmelon.com.au/ns/Tour%20-%20Encrypting%20Private%20Data.shtml. Accessed 2004.

Figure 6-1   Note Studio encrypts data and hides files.

Event Logging

Logging is necessary to maintain security for Web applications, their associated processes, and their integrated technologies. Transaction logs are necessary for many reasons, including the following:

- Logs are frequently the only record of suspicious behavior taking place, and they can sometimes feed immediately and directly into intrusion detection systems.

- Logs can, in some situations, be required in legal actions to confirm illegal behavior. This makes the actual handling of the log data critical.

- Logs are used to reconstruct an event after any problem has occurred, security related or otherwise. The reconstruction of an event can permit a security administrator to discover the full extent of an intruder's behavior and accelerate the recovery process.

What to Log

Each log entry should include suitable debugging information such as the time of the event, the initiating process, the owner of the process, and a brief description of the event. The following events should be logged:

- Reading and writing data
- Modification of any characteristics, including access control permissions, position in database or file system, or ownership
- Deletion of data objects
- Network communications at all positions (bind, connect, accept, etc.)
- Authentication events (logging in, logging out, failed logins, etc.)
- Each administrative action, regardless of overlap (account management actions, seeing any user's data, enabling or disabling logging, etc.)
- Various debugging information that can be enabled or disabled on the fly

Log Management

Log security is very important, because if logs can be compromised, they become useless for after-the-fact security analysis or legal prosecution. Logs should be composed and consolidated on a separate, devoted logging host. To protect privacy and integrity, the network connections or actual log data content should be encrypted.

Every logging station should be synchronized with a time server. This time server should be hardened and should not provide any other services to the network.

Logs should also be written to a write-once/read-many device, like a CD-ROM, for added security. At regular intervals, copies of log files should be made. Common naming conventions should be used to make logs easier to index. The log files should be copied and moved to permanent storage and integrated into the organization's overall backup policy.

For more information on log management, see Chapter 5.

Embedded Application Security

Embedded technology is playing an increasingly vital role in higher-end applications. Most devices transfer data using the connection-oriented TCP/IP. This enhances system efficiency to a great extent. However, attackers can capture these data packets from the network and then manipulate them. Intruders can also gain access to networked equipment.

Embedded devices are mostly used in network environments to handle a large number of critical transactions. This leaves them open to threats and vulnerabilities. Some main problems include computationally intensive cryptography algorithms and significant memory requirements for adequate security. However, hardware technology is advancing, and cryptographic algorithms and separate protocols are being developed specifically for embedded systems.

TCP/IP Security Technology

TCP/IP is the most commonly used communications protocol, which means it is well known and particularly vulnerable to attacks. Most attackers and intruders accomplish their goals by attacking TCP/IP packets. These packets can be traced, captured, and manipulated from the Internet. This makes it difficult to use large IP networks for sensitive communications.

IPSec and SSL Security

Various TCP/IP security protocols are used in preventing threats and vulnerabilities. The most popularly used are IP security (IPSec) and Secure Sockets Layer (SSL). Additional security protocols include Data Encryption Standard (DES), Advanced Encryption Standard (AES), Message Digest 5 (MD5), and Secure Hashing Algorithm (SHA).

SSL works at the transport layer of a TCP/IP stack, between the TCP and UDP layers and the application layer. It is used to provide secure authentication to Web applications. It works at the transport layer where few applications interact, such as Web, e-mail, and file transfer applications.

IPSec works in a lower part of the stack, in the network layer. It provides secured authentication and is easily operable with applications such as Web, e-mail, and file transfer applications as well as terminal services, IP telephony, and other client-server applications. It also works with UDP-based applications, such as audio and video streaming.

SSL and IPSec provide the same kind of encryption and authentication mechanisms. However, IPSec is more secure than SSL due to the following features:

- Specially configured software on both the client and server side is an essential prerequisite for IPSec.
- IPSec secures more detailed information than SSL, while SSL guarantees that the data portion will only have TCP information.
- IPSec uses techniques such as tunneling to conceal full user details.

IPSec and SSL in Embedded Systems IPSec and SSL protocols greatly enhance the security of embedded devices, mainly power-sensitive microprocessors. SSL is widely adopted at the server side with embedded devices and can be accessed by users with a standard Web browser. There must be a standard interface due to the integration of SSL-based applications with the SSL socket layer.

IPSec is mainly used on the client side to make connections with a virtual private network (VPN). With IPSec, no standard Web browser is needed due to fewer changes made at the socket layer. Because embedded devices have very complicated, computationally intensive algorithms, these protocols can be implemented for low-power, memory-constrained, and embedded devices.

Network Security for Embedded Applications

Security for embedded systems is more difficult than for desktop and enterprise computing. The importance of universal connectivity for embedded systems increases the possibility for malicious users to obtain unauthorized access to confidential information. Modern security protocols include private-key and public-key encryption algorithms, such as RC4, AES, and RSA. Figure 6-2 shows network security for embedded applications.

Embedded Network Security Hardware Instructions

To deal with the functional and memory-related problems of deploying network security in embedded systems, many solutions have been devised to merge network security hardware instructions into embedded processor cores. As a result, these instructions increase the speed and efficiency of embedded security algorithms.

Software stacks for security protocols benefit from these hardware instructions. Outputs of the protocol stack have been developed to use the memory in the embedded systems as efficiently as possible.

These instructions can be expandable, giving developers choices for which features are suitable for a specific application. Client-side-only or server-side-only configurations are supported based on the requirements of the system.

The IPShield security protocol stack is an extension of IPSec for OEMs aiming to include security and VPN functionality in their Internet infrastructure. IPShield uses Internet Key Exchange (IKE) software to cautiously interchange encryption and authentication keys. The stack is in compliance with a wide range of cryptographic algorithms including DES, Triple DES, MD5, SHA, and AES.

Figure 6-3 shows embedded network security hardware instructions.

Remote Administration Security Implementation

Remote access to Web sites creates a server security threat, in that it can be difficult to control fraudulent access. Web page editors like Microsoft FrontPage make it easy to create Web sites, but they also make them more vulnerable to modifications. FrontPage has the ability to easily alter Web settings, which can be misused to modify or even delete the sites. To prevent the modification of Web sites by unauthorized persons, the following preventive measures should be taken:

- Use a protected connection when communicating with Fpadmdll.dll and Fpadmcgi.exe. This ensures that the file configurations, usernames, and passwords that are passed over the Internet are not hacked, and also prevents unauthorized users from falsely utilizing administrative privileges.

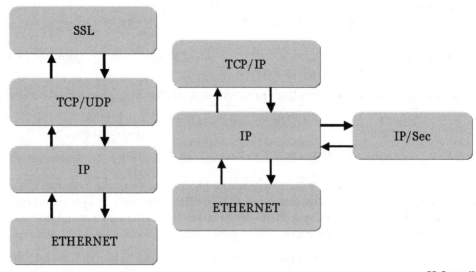

Figure 6-2   This chart shows network security for embedded applications.

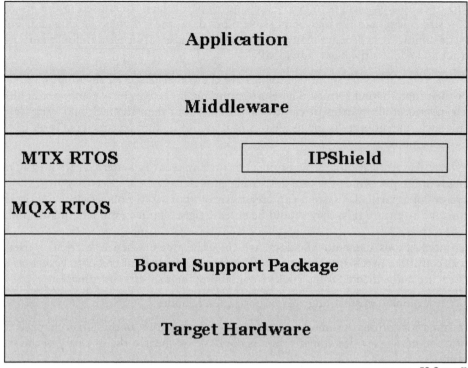

Figure 6-3 Embedded network security hardware instructions can increase the speed and efficiency of embedded security algorithms.

- Use a nonstandard HTTP port in order to make it more difficult for intruders to identify the port used to access administrative privileges, forms, and programs.
- Restricting IP addresses can prevent computers that are not authenticated from gaining access to HTML administration forms and files. The servers requesting access should be monitored to detect unidentified computers trying to access important information.
- Operating systems like UNIX and Microsoft Windows NT can use a utility called Fpsrvadm to protect FrontPage applications.
- Fpremadm is another application to administer FrontPage Server Extensions. This can be used at the command line to remotely access Windows-enabled servers.
- The HTML administration forms for FrontPage can be copied to the server's hard disk during setup. These forms help to administer the FrontPage Extensions remotely and securely.

Secure Coding

Most experienced software professionals claim that it is literally impossible to build a totally secure system. Software is always prone to virus attacks. Therefore, when developing software, the goal is to make it as strong as possible against viruses and attacks. The budget required to develop such software can be high, which causes added difficulty.

Common Software Errors

Even amateur hackers can easily access hacking programs from the Internet with very little effort. Because of this, it is imperative that software errors be fixed as soon as they are found.

Buffer Overflow This is a commonly made error by most programmers and has proven very useful to hackers. Buffer overflows are caused when a variable with a fixed size is used to store input into the system. If a hacker puts more data into that variable than it is meant to hold, that could allow the hacker to rewrite other system values.

The way to track this problem is to verify the lengths of all the buffers used in the program. If it is found that the buffer size is less than the highest possible input data, the size must be changed. This correction may be very time consuming, but there are many tools to make it easier. Still, the developer must again scan through the final output and address the bugs individually.

Format-String Vulnerabilities Format strings are the constructs used in programming languages like C and C++ for their input/output format. These programming languages have some special identifiers. If certain input is given in susceptible systems, it can disclose data about the call stack and variables used in routines. The source for such susceptibility is the usage of variables in function parameters. Tools can be used to detect format-string vulnerabilities.

Authentication Authentication is a major concern for any security system. A frequently made error during authenticating is to use passwords that are not strong enough to prevent a security attack.

Administrators of a particular system can create custom password policies. It is important that passwords be very secure, and to ensure this, they should be at least eight characters in length and contain alphanumeric and special characters.

Some Web applications use authenticators, which authenticate when a particular user enters a system. Authenticators confirm a user's authenticity by using tickets rather than credentials such as the username and password. Users are authenticated using cookies containing their specific information.

Authorization Common mistakes during authorization include:

- *Imperfect authorization:* In some cases, the system assumes that nothing has changed if a user has been authenticated in the past. If authentication is not done frequently, the integrity of the system is lost to an extent.

- *Unsubstantiated trust of the input data:* In some cases, whatever data is being inputted is not scrutinized adequately, such as usernames and passwords that are presumed to be verified. Hackers find it simple to hack a system in these situations by periodically entering the same existing data.

- *Errors due to multiple depictions of the data:* Data can be depicted in multiple forms and many users may not be aware that the desired output can be achieved through many different query methods, including different formats and path names. This can allow hackers to hack systems without the knowledge of authorized users.

Cryptography Cryptography is implemented to provide security for files and information transfers. Some cryptography techniques use complex mathematics, which can make them difficult to use. Some cryptographic algorithms are developed for one specific organization and work only to protect that particular system. If any flaws occur in the development of such a specific algorithm, it can destroy the security of the whole organization.

To prevent losses from situations where users think data is safely encrypted, but it is actually not, it is always advisable to use the services of some other outside organization. CryptoAPI and CAPICOM installed within Windows solve such problems.

Guidelines for Secure Coding

When developing software, it is important to conduct tests, reviews, and audits to trace the bugs in the system. The following sections describe guidelines that should be followed to prevent many issues from arising in the first place.

Distrust User Input Most hacking in Web applications takes place through external gateways to the applications, which are known as *interfaces*. Some of the types of interfaces include sockets, Web forms, command-line input, and files. Many hackers try to send corrupted input data, which may result in the system behaving in an unpredictable manner. A good example of malicious user input is the buffer overflow attack.

Input Validation For most Web applications, a hacker can guess what software and protocols the majority of users use. They may attempt to hack Web applications through other means, such as by using Web browsers that are not used extensively by the majority of users.

Malicious Code Detection An important point in detecting malicious code is focusing on the system's network behavior. An administrator can determine what services are being provided on the device and perform a port scan. He or she can also run a packet sniffer on the device.

The system of malicious code detection includes the following:

- Front-end processor, which gets a flow of content from an external network and provides the flow to each scanning computer system

- Multiple scanning computer systems, which watch the traffic for malicious code and produce an alarm when malicious code is identified

- Detection management system, which will take action against the flow if an alarm is produced by at least one scanning computer system

Programming Standards and Controls

Most programmers mainly focus on functionality and make security a secondary priority. This creates a problem for everyone depending on the software they develop and puts a huge liability on the developers.

Change Controls Change control is a procedure that handles or controls the authorized changes to an organization's assets such as software and hardware. It also checks for the access privileges of users on the network, processes of the business, etc. It involves the mechanisms of change requests, results recording, documenting, testing the results after the changes, and gaining approval for the requests. Change controls detail procedures for analyzing problems, updating the results, and sending a request for change to the appropriate personnel. This is reviewed, and authorization for the change is given only if the change is required.

Internal Labeling An internal label is used to identify the following:

- Starting point of development

- Development code baseline implemented in a regular periodic build/compile of an application

- Development baseline from a nonerror build that is used for packaging and testing

- A deliverable targeted for testing and the corresponding development code baseline

- The bug fixes required to correct release deliverables that are in production

Threat Modeling for Web Applications

Threat modeling is a structured activity to identify threats and vulnerabilities in applications. This section uses a question-driven approach for threat modeling, which helps to identify security design problems in the application design process.

The threat modeling approach is used to focus on identifying and addressing vulnerabilities. The security objectives, threats, and attacks found in the early steps of the approach are designed to help find vulnerabilities in the application.

Threat modeling helps to:

- Identify relevant threats to a particular application scenario

- Identify key vulnerabilities in application design

- Improve security design

When using this approach, an administrator should keep the following in mind:

- Try not to get stuck on specific steps or implementations; focus on the approach. If any step becomes impassable, go right to Step 4 and identify the problem.

- Use scenarios to scope the modeling activity.

- Use existing design documents. Make use of items like documented use cases or user stories, architecture diagrams, data flow diagrams, and other design documentation.

- Start with a whiteboard before capturing information in documents or getting lost in details. It may be helpful to use a digital camera with printing capabilities to document and distribute the information from the whiteboard.
- Use an iterative approach. Add more details and improve the threat model as design and development continue. This will help you become familiar with the modeling process and develop the threat model to better examine more possible scenarios.
- Obtain input about host and network constraints from system and network administrators. To better understand the end-to-end deployment diagram, obtain as much information as possible about host configurations, firewall policies, allowed protocols and ports, etc.

Step 1: Identify Security Objectives

Security objectives are the goals and constrains related to the application's confidentiality, integrity, and availability. Security-specific objectives guide the threat modeling efforts. To identify security objectives, administrators should ask the following questions:

- What client data must be protected?
- Are there any compliance requirements?
- Are there specific quality-of-service requirements?
- Are there intangible assets that must be protected?

Step 2: Create an Application Overview

This step helps the administrator understand what the Web application will do. It is important to identify the application's key functionality, characteristics, and clients in order to identify relevant threats in Step 4.

Draw the End-To-End Deployment Scenario

To draw the end-to-end deployment scenario, the administrator should use a whiteboard. First, he or she should draw a rough diagram that explains the working and structure of the application, its subsystems, and its deployment characteristics. The deployment diagram should contain the following:

- End-to-end deployment topology
- Logical layers
- Key components
- Key services
- Communication ports and protocols
- Identities
- External dependencies

Identify Roles

The administrator should identify who can do what within the application. What can users do? Are there higher-privileged groups of users? For example, who can read data, who can update data, and who can delete data?

Identify Key Usage Scenarios

The administrator uses the application's usage cases to determine the application's objective. Key scenarios also described in usage cases explain how the application is used and how it is misused.

Identify Technologies

The administrator should list the technologies and key features of the software, as well as the following:

- Operating systems
- Web server software
- Database server software

- Technologies used in the presentation, business, and data access layers
- Development languages

Identifying these technologies helps to focus on technology-specific threats.

Identify Application Security Mechanisms

The administrator should identify any key points regarding the following:

- Input and data validation
- Authorization
- Authentication
- Sensitive data
- Configuration management
- Session management
- Parameter manipulation
- Cryptography
- Exception management
- Auditing and logging

The aim of these efforts is to identify relevant details and be able to add details where required, or to identify where more research is required.

Step 3: Decompose the Application

In this step, the administrator breaks down the application to identify trust boundaries, data flows, entry points, and exit points. This makes it considerably easier to identify threats and vulnerabilities.

Identify Trust Boundaries

Identifying the application's trust boundaries helps the administrator focus on the relevant areas of the application. It indicates where trust levels change.

To help identify trust boundaries, the administrator should do the following:

- Identify outer system boundaries
- Identify access control points, or key places where access requires extra privileges or role membership
- Identify trust boundaries from a data flow perspective

Identify Data Flows

The administrator should list the application's data input from entry to exit. This helps him or her understand how the application communicates with outside systems and clients, and how internal components interact. He or she should pay particular attention to the data flow across the trust boundaries and how it is validated at the trust boundary entry point. A good approach is to start at the highest level and then deconstruct the application by testing the data flow between different subsystems.

Identify Entry Points

The application's entry point can also serve as an entry point for attacks. These entry points are designed to be exposed to clients. Other internal entry points uncovered by subcomponents over the layers of the application may be present only to support internal communication with other components. The administrator should identify these entry points to determine the methods used by an intruder to get in through them. He or she should focus on the entry points that allow access to critical functionalities and provide adequate defense for them.

Identify Exit Points

The administrator should also identify the points where the application transfers data to the client or external system. He or she should prioritize exit points where the application writes data containing client input or data from untrusted sources, like a shared database.

Step 4: Identify Threats

The administrator should bring members of the development and test teams together to identify potential threats. The team should start with a list of common threats grouped by application vulnerability categories. This step uses a question-driven approach to help identify threats.

Identify Common Threats and Attacks

The team should ask the following questions to identify common threats and attacks:

- Authentication
  - How could an attacker spoof identity?
  - How could an attacker get access to the credential store?
  - How could an attacker mount a dictionary attack? How are users' credentials stored and what password policies are enforced?
  - How can an attacker modify, intercept, or bypass a user's credential reset mechanism?
- Authorization
  - How could an attacker influence authorization checks to gain access to privileged operations?
  - How could an attacker elevate privileges?
- Sensitive data
  - Where and how does the application store sensitive data?
  - When and where is sensitive data passed across the network?
  - How could an attacker view sensitive data?
  - How could an attacker manipulate sensitive data?
- Configuration management
  - How could an attacker gain access to administration functionality?
  - How could an attacker gain access to the application's configuration data?
- Input and data validation
  - How could an attacker inject SQL commands?
  - How could an attacker perform a cross-site scripting attack?
  - How could an attacker bypass input validation?
  - How could an attacker send invalid input to influence security logic on the server?
  - How could an attacker send malformed input to crash the application?
- Cryptography
  - What would it take for an attacker to crack the encryption?
  - How could an attacker obtain access to encryption keys?
  - Which cryptographic standards are used? What, if any, are the known attacks on these standards?
  - How might the deployment topology impact the choice of encryption methods?
- Session management
  - Is the encryption algorithm trustworthy?
  - How could an attacker hijack a session?
  - How could an attacker view or manipulate another user's session state?
- Exception management
  - How could an attacker crash the application?
  - How could an attacker gain useful exception details?

- Parameter manipulation
  - How could an attacker manipulate parameters to influence security logic on the server?
  - How could an attacker manipulate sensitive parameter data?
- Auditing and logging
  - How could an attacker cover his or her tracks?
  - How can it be proven what actions an attacker took?

Identify Threats Along Usage Cases

The team should check every application's key usage case and check the way in which a user can innocently cause the application to make an unauthorized operation or to reveal confidential or private data. The team should ask the following questions:

- How can a client inject malicious input?
- Is data being written out based on user input or on invalidated user input?
- How could an attacker manipulate session data?
- How could an attacker obtain sensitive data as it is passed over the network?
- How could an attacker bypass authorization checks?

Identify Threats Along Data Flows

The team should examine the data flow between different components in the architecture as well as the usage cases. When identifying threats associated with data flows, the team should ask the following questions:

- How does data flow from the front end to the back end of the application?
- How does valid data look?
- Where is validation performed?
- How are the data constrained?
- How are data validated against the expected length, range, format, and type?
- What sensitive data are passed between components and across networks, and how are those data secured while in transit?

Step 5: Identify Vulnerabilities

In this step, the administrator reviews the Web application security framework and specifically searches for vulnerabilities, not threats. He or she focuses on the vulnerability types. The questions given in this section are designed to help identify vulnerabilities.

Authentication

The administrator identifies authentication vulnerabilities by asking the following:

- Are usernames and passwords sent in plaintext over an unprotected channel? Is any ad hoc cryptography used for sensitive information?
- Are credentials stored? If they are stored, how are they stored and protected?
- Are strong passwords enforced? What other password policies are enforced?
- How are credentials verified?
- How is the authenticated user identified after the initial logon?

Authentication can be reviewed by looking for these common vulnerabilities:

- Sending authentication information or authentication cookies over unencrypted network links, which can result in credential capture or session hijacking
- Using weak password and account policies
- Combining privacy with authentication

Authorization

The administrator identifies authorization vulnerabilities by asking the following:

- What access controls are used at the entry points of the application?
- Does the application use roles? If it uses roles, are they sufficiently granular for access control and auditing purposes?
- Does the authorization code fail securely and grant access only upon the successful confirmation of credentials?
- Is access to system resources restricted?
- Is database access restricted?
- How is authorization enforced at the database?

The administrator reviews authorization by looking for these common vulnerabilities:

- Using overprivileged roles and accounts
- Failing to provide sufficient role granularity
- Failing to restrict system resources to particular application identities

Configuration Management

The administrator identifies configuration management vulnerabilities by asking the following:

- How are remote administration interfaces protected?
- Are configuration stores protected?
- Are sensitive configuration data protected?
- Are administrator privileges separated?
- Are least-privileged process and service accounts used?

The administrator reviews configuration management by looking for these common vulnerabilities:

- Storing configuration secrets, such as connection strings and service-account credentials, in plaintext
- Failing to protect the configuration management aspects of the application, including administration interfaces
- Using overprivileged process accounts and service accounts

Input and Data Validation

The administrator identifies input and data validation vulnerabilities by asking the following questions:

- Are all input data validated?
- Are they validated for length, range, format, and type?
- Is there only client-side validation?
- Could an attacker inject commands or malicious data into the application?
- Are data written out to Web pages trustworthy, or do they need to be HTML-encoded to help prevent cross-site scripting attacks?
- Is input validated before being used in SQL statements to help prevent SQL injection?
- Are data validated at the recipient entry point as they are passed between separate trust boundaries?
- Can data in the database be trusted?
- Are input filename, URLs, or usernames accepted?
- Have canonicalization issues been addressed?

The administrator reviews input validation by looking for these common vulnerabilities:

- Relying exclusively on client-side validation
- Using a *deny* approach instead of an *allow* approach for filtering input

- Writing nonvalidated data to Web pages
- Using nonvalidated input to generate SQL queries
- Using insecure data access coding techniques, which can increase the threat posed by SQL injection
- Using input filenames, URLs, or usernames for security decisions

Sensitive Data

The administrator identifies sensitive data vulnerabilities by asking the following:

- Are secrets in persistent stores?
- How is sensitive data stored?
- Is confidential information stored in memory?
- How are sensitive data passed over the network?
- Are sensitive data logged?

The administrator reviews sensitive data by looking for these common vulnerabilities:

- Storing confidential information when it does not need to be stored
- Storing secrets in code
- Storing secrets in plaintext
- Passing sensitive data in plaintext over networks

Session Management

The administrator identifies session management vulnerabilities by asking the following:

- How are session cookies generated?
- How are session identifiers exchanged?
- How is the session state protected as it crosses the network?
- How is the session state protected to prevent session hijacking?
- How is the session state store protected?
- Is a session lifetime restricted?
- How does the application authenticate with the session store?
- Are credentials passed over the network and are they maintained by the application? If they are, how are they protected?

The administrator reviews session management by looking for these common vulnerabilities:

- Passing session identifiers over unencrypted channels
- Prolonged session lifetime
- Insecure session state stores
- Session identifiers in query strings

Parameter Manipulation

The administrator identifies parameter manipulation vulnerabilities by asking the following:

- Are all input parameters validated?
- Are all parameters validated in form fields, view states, cookie data, and HTTP headers?
- Are sensitive data passed in parameters?
- Does the application detect parameter tampering?

The administrator reviews parameter manipulation by looking for these common vulnerabilities:

- Failing to validate all input parameters, making the application susceptible to denial-of-service attacks and code injection attacks, including SQL injection and XSS

- Including sensitive data in unencrypted cookies, which can be changed at the client or captured and changed as they are passed over the network
- Including sensitive data in query strings and form fields, which are easily changed on the client
- Trusting HTTP header information, which is easily changed on the client

Cryptography

The administrator identifies cryptography vulnerabilities by asking the following:

- What algorithms and cryptographic techniques are used?
- Are custom encryption algorithms used?
- Why are particular algorithms used?
- How long are encryption keys and how are they protected?
- How often are keys recycled?
- How are encryption keys distributed?

The administrator reviews cryptography by looking for these common vulnerabilities:

- Using custom cryptography
- Using the wrong algorithm or a key size that is too small
- Failing to protect encryption keys
- Using the same key for a prolonged period of time

Exception Management

The administrator identifies exception management vulnerabilities by asking the following:

- How does the application handle error conditions?
- Are exceptions ever allowed to propagate back to the client?
- What data is included in exception messages?
- Is too much information revealed to the client?
- Where are exception details logged? Are the log files secure?

The administrator reviews exception management by looking for these common vulnerabilities:

- Failing to validate all input parameters
- Revealing too much information to the client

Auditing and Logging

The administrator identifies auditing and logging vulnerabilities by asking the following:

- Have key activities to audit been identified?
- Does the application audit activity across all layers and servers?
- How are log files protected?

The administrator reviews auditing and logging by looking for these common vulnerabilities:

- Failing to audit failed logons
- Failing to protect audit files
- Failing to audit across application layers and servers

Chapter Summary

- The main problems with Web security involve managing Web browser activity.
- A threat is the occurrence of any event or circumstance that could harm assets.
- SQL injection attacks inject malicious commands into SQL database queries.
- Administrators should be sure to allow users to only use the resources that they need and place a security checkpoint before users are allowed to perform any sensitive application-related function.
- Elevation of privileges involves an attacker gaining the privileges of the local administrator to have full control over the machine or system.
- A luring attack is one in which a lower-privileged user tricks a higher-privileged component into running a process that performs malicious activities.
- When using Web applications, security is extremely important because data regularly flow in and out of the network, and these data must be protected.
- Every session token must be unique, nonpredictable, and resistant to reverse engineering.
- Embedded devices are mostly used in network environments to handle a large number of critical transactions, leaving the devices open to threats and vulnerabilities.
- TCP/IP is the most commonly used communications protocol, which means it is well known and particularly vulnerable to attacks.
- Threat modeling is a structured activity to identify threats and vulnerabilities in applications.

Review Questions

1. What are some common application threats?

2. What are some commonly used methods of cracking passwords?

3. What are the countermeasures for cross-site scripting?

4. What are the countermeasures for SQL injection?

5. What are configuration management threats, and how are they countered?

_____

_____

_____

_____

6. What is the difference between secure and nonsecure cookies?

_____

_____

_____

_____

7. What are the benefits of event logging?

_____

_____

_____

_____

8. What is the function of IPSec and SSL in embedded systems?

_____

_____

_____

_____

9. What is the process for remote administrator security?

_____

_____

_____

_____

10. What are the five steps of threat modeling?

_____

_____

_____

_____

Hands-On Projects

1. Read about the top 10 Web application vulnerabilities.

   ▓ Navigate to Chapter 6 of the Student Resource Center.

   ▓ Open OWASP_Top_10_2007.pdf and read the content.

2. Read about web application security.

   ▓ Navigate to Chapter 6 of the Student Resource Center.

   ▓ Open Web Application Security 101.pdf and read the content.

3. Read about Web security threats.

   ▓ Navigate to Chapter 6 of the Student Resource Center.

   ▓ Open WebSecurityThreats.pdf and read the content.

4. Read why Web application security is important.

   ▓ Navigate to Chapter 6 of the Student Resource Center.

   ▓ Open Why Web Application Security is Important.pdf and read the content.

5. Read about the need for Web application security.

   ▓ Navigate to Chapter 6 of the Student Resource Center.

   ▓ Open Zanero-BH-Amsterdam-05.pdf and read the content.

6. Read about threats and countermeasures.

   ▓ Navigate to Chapter 6 of the Student Resource Center.

   ▓ Open Threats_Countermeasures.pdf and read the content.

Index